L
THOUSAND
ISLANDS
INDONESIA

AMITABHA GANGOPADHYAY

INDIA · SINGAPORE · MALAYSIA

ISBN 979-8-89026-680-4

Contents

Acknowledgement

To Desi, Kadek, Ninik, Gonzalez and all my guides in Indonesia,

You all made sure that every step of my journey in your beautiful country was safe. You taught me how to love Indonesia. I will remain grateful to you forever.

To my father,

You taught me how to dream a dream. I will try to turn my dreams into reality all my life. That will be my true learning from you.

This book is a tribute to all of you!

This is how it began!

The Tiger Air flight took off on time from Changi Airport in Singapore. Destination Bali! It was just over a two-hour journey to Bali from Singapore. Once the seat belt sign was turned off, I inclined my seat and relaxed. It was a bright sunny afternoon. The aircraft took a wide turn over the South China Sea and headed towards Indonesia. I let out a deep sigh of relief.

"Finally, it's happening. I am travelling to Bali!" I thought.

Indonesia has been on my bucket list for quite some time now. Once I attempted to travel there while touring Vietnam but I had to scrap the plan as there was not enough time on my hands. There was so much to see in Indonesia that a 'touch and go' trip did not make any sense. The country stretches over 5000 km from east to west and I wanted to explore it at my pace. So, the next time, I planned the trip well ahead of time and I must say that it was not easy. Other than spending some time in Bali and other tourist destinations, I also wanted to travel to some unfrequented paths. I am never satisfied by spending all my time in popular tourist destinations. I thrive on meeting the locals and travelling beyond the usual city limits where I feel at home. Moreover, I must admit I love to feel the touch of wilderness and the taste of adventure. I guess that is in my blood since I was a boy. So the desire to encounter the near-extinct Komodo dragons on a remote island far away in the Java Sea and to chase some orangutans in the deep Borneo jungle fit perfectly into my wish list, but it was not easy to fit into a typical tourist itinerary. Planning for this trip to Indonesia was getting complicated. I had a tough time finding reliable sources in Indonesia who would take me to those places safely. As I relaxed during my flight and looked out of the window at the turquoise-blue Java Sea below, I thought back on how it all finally took shape.

Let's rewind a couple of months. In early March, a very good deal on airfare popped up in my inbox. 'All Nippon Airways' announced a flash sale for travelling to South East Asia in November. It was a cool deal; it included a bit of hopping flights here and there to finally reach Bali which was not so bad. So I quickly grabbed it and let it sit for a while. Meanwhile, in Calgary, summer came and slowly faded into a soft fall season. One Sunday morning, the changing seasons reminded me it was time for my trip. I needed to get ready. I started looking for my backpack after breakfast.

My wife noticed that I was searching through our luggage stack in the closet and asked, "What are you looking for?"

"Umm… my backpack, you know," I replied.

"Aha, time for your adventure, I guess," she grinned.

"Not yet. It is early winter. I am just getting my gear ready."

"Where are you heading to this time?"

"Indonesia, for sure! There is plenty to see."

"Bali?"

"That's the hub," I paused for a moment and then said, "But you know, I stay away from the tourist spots."

"I heard that it's really nice over there."

"You are right, I heard that too. I will touch Bali, but I will make it a hub for travelling to other places."

"Like what?"

"Borobudur Temple for sure. It's a historic landmark. But there is something else," I paused.

Yes, there was something else! Bali is nice and Borobudur is a 'must-see' place, but the outback and adventure were in my blood. I thrive on them. The Borneo wilderness had attracted me like a magnet since my childhood. I had wanted to set foot there for such a long time. When I started travelling to South East Asia, I often toyed with the idea of making a side trip to Borneo. The vast region of Kalimantan is mostly inhabited by the Dayak tribe. Indeed, it had been on my wish list for a long time and I longed to explore it.

"Go on," she said, waiting for me. "I'm listening."

I looked at her and replied, "Well, I would like to spend some time in the Borneo jungle, trekking through the wilderness and searching for orangutans, you know."

"Orangutans? That seems exciting."

"You bet! You wanna come?"

"Having one monkey at home is enough for me!" she laughed.

"Ha ha ha, funny!"

"That's it?"

"I am also thinking of adding Komodo and Rinca islands to the agenda."

"What's there?"

"Komodo dragons and they are on the verge of extinction."

"Dragons! Couldn't you find any other species to go on a date with? How about a dinosaur?" she laughed again.

"Come on, now! You know me. I love adventures."

"Yeah, yeah! You and your adventures! Be careful though. These dragons may like you too much and keep you there!" she smiled and left.

So, Borneo it was! And the rest of the trip was jelling in.

"Desi, I want to plan a day trip to Komodo and Rinca islands," I said.

Desi was my tour organizer from Adventure Indonesia in Bali. She was a cheerful, easy-going Balinese girl. I was lucky to find her. We had become friends in a short time.

"That's in the Java Sea. Do you really wanna go there?"

"Yup! I am looking for Komodo dragons!"

"Aaha! No worries, you don't have to look for them, they will look for you," she laughed over the phone.

"Cut it out! Can you fix it, please? And preferably a day trip."

"Are you kidding? No way! You can't make it on a day trip. You need to fly in and out of Labuan Bajo from Bali. Then you have to take a four-hour boat ride each way to Komodo island from Labuan Bajo. You need at least two full days if not three."

"Ok, will do. But please arrange the flights and the boat ride."

"Sure thing! Please call me in a couple of days."

"What about the tours in Bali and Ubud?"

"Those are simple. Consider it done! No worries."

Yogyakarta and Borneo were the last two trips that needed to be fixed. Yogyakarta is a tourist destination and that wouldn't be much of a problem. But Borneo was a different matter. First of all, it was not close to Bali at all. As a matter of fact, it was on the other side of Bali, on the east coast of Indonesia. That was not the only problem. The deep swamps in Borneo were filled with crocodiles, and its miles of dense woods were full of mosquitoes, snakes and other not-so-friendly species that make it difficult to navigate. It was not a typical tourist destination. So I was not quite sure how Desi would handle it. I did mention it to her a couple of times, but she hadn't come up with a solution yet.

"Give me a call in a couple of days, please," she said and hung up the phone.

If Desi was not able to fix my trip to Borneo, I was not even sure how to get there. So, I waited for a few days and gave her a call.

"It's done, my friend… well mostly, I should say," replied Desi, in her usual cheerful voice.

"Go on!"

"I have made some progress. The rest of the arrangements can be discussed when you are here in Bali. I am not there yet. But trust me, I will work something out!" she said and went off the line.

That's pretty much how Desi summed up the trip for me. It didn't leave me with a warm and fuzzy feeling. But I trusted her.

"*So be it, let's go with the flow. She knows what she is doing*," I thought as I continued packing that Sunday morning.

One:

Everyone loves Bali

Sharing my moments in Bali

The Tiger Air flight made a smooth touchdown at Denpasar airport in a fading twilight. There was a downpour just before we landed. From my window seat, I could see the water splash from the touchdown. Beyond the runway, a brilliant golden sun was peeping out from the edge of the cloud before touching the horizon over the Indian Ocean. Its sparkling rays were reflected on the rain-soaked runway. The plane taxied slowly to the terminal. The single-story bungalow-style terminal building with red tiles looked very neat. Bali!

"This is where I start my journey," I mused.

Obviously, I was excited. Months of planning, emails and phone calls had finally brought me to this part of the world where thousands of people set foot to embrace Bali's culture and have some fun. Yes, I was one of them! Over the last six months, Desi and I had meticulously planned a bucketful of activities in Bali. Of course, I would have some fun with paragliding and various other water sports but that was just to quench my thirst for an adrenaline rush and was only one part of my journey. As I said, the part of Bali that truly attracted me was its rich culture and old history of Hinduism. I wanted to feel the vibe of how the locals lived their daily life. I also wanted to visit the temples and get a taste of the Ubud livelihood.

I was interested in learning how Hinduism from India had migrated to Bali and blended here with Balinese culture. I learned a bit of Bahasa to carry out some basic communication with the locals although most people in Bali can speak English. Interestingly, the Bahasa language itself was developed from the ancient Indian language Sanskrit (the word 'Bhasha' in Sanskrit means 'language'). So I had a lot to learn from the Balinese. Unfortunately, my stay in Bali would be only for three days and it would be a daunting task to explore such details in such a short time. To be honest, one can only scratch the surface during such a short stay.

"Oh, well… I will do the best I can," I told myself.

The immigration process was slow and the officers were chatting casually with their colleagues, cracking jokes and having a laugh while processing papers. The atmosphere was totally relaxed. We were used to seeing the hard faces of immigration officers upon landing in North America, but not in Bali. Cool! It was a different world altogether. Desi and Ayu would be waiting for me at the airport. They worked in 'Adventure Indonesia.' Desi looked after marketing and Ayu was from the accounts department. I had talked to Desi over the phone many times, but I had no clue what she looked like. However, it didn't take me long to figure that out when we met in the arrival lounge. She couldn't hide her usual laugh which I was used to. We drove to my hotel in Nusa Dua where Desi's boyfriend Kadek was waiting for us. He had come directly from work to meet us. First things first! I worked with Ayu to settle my outstanding dues after our initial excitement was over. Once that was sorted out, Ayu left and I quickly checked in. I dumped my luggage in my room and returned to the lobby where Desi and Kadek were waiting for me. And woo-hoo, the party began! Both of them were easygoing and a lot of fun.

"Shall we grab some dinner?" suggested Desi.

Not a bad idea, I was getting a bit hungry.

"What would you fancy eating tonight?" asked Kadek, turning to me.

"*Not a bad idea, perhaps I can taste some local cuisine*," I thought.

"How about some local food?" I asked.

"Nasi Goreng?"

"What about it?"

"It's an Indonesian rice dish. It is actually fried rice with meat and vegetables," replied Desi.

"I'm fine with that, but I will skip the spices. Sorry, travel rules! No rich food while travelling."

"Hey, not to worry, we will tell the owner to make it less spicy."

We settled for some Nasi Goreng at a roadside stall and kept chatting as the evening rolled into the night. I had no idea that we had so much to share.

"It is the right company!" I thought.

But they had a long ride home to Sanur which was north of Bali. I too had a busy day ahead. So we called it a night.

The next day, I got up early in the morning. This was a standard travel ritual for me and allows me to cover a whole lot of things. I checked my watch. It was 6 am. By the time I finished my breakfast, Sudana was already waiting for me in the hotel lobby with the car. Desi had arranged for him to show me around Bali and Ubud. In short, he would be my guide and chauffeur. The plan was to drive to Besakih Temple first thing in the morning. It's the largest temple in Bali. I still recall the argument that I had with Desi while planning the trip. My flight was scheduled to arrive in Bali on the evening of 25th November. Desi had booked me for paragliding at noon the following day. So my morning was free. When I suggested that I visit the Besakih Temple in the morning, Desi freaked out.

"You are kidding! You are just arriving in Bali on the evening of the 25th. You can't visit both Besakih Temple and go paragliding in a single day. That's insane!"

"Why can't I go to Besakih Temple in the morning? I am free."

"Oh, you are like a little kid! You know, the temple is far away from Nusa Dua where you are staying and there is traffic on the road. If you leave even at 8:00 am, you can't possibly come back on time for paragliding."

Desi was advising me from her experience. Bali is a tourist hotspot and the traffic could back up for hours. Heading out somewhere during rush hour meant that one needed to plan, keeping ample time in hand. But I was boneheaded and did not budge from my plan.

"I sure can. We will leave at 6 am."

"You are crazy! Why don't you relax in the morning before you head out for paragliding?"

"I relax all year round. You don't know me, Desi. Four to five hours of sleep is good enough for me. We will leave at 6 am and be back on time for paragliding. Will you please just arrange a car for me?"

Desi sighed and gave up while saying, "It's your call, but you are pushing it. I wouldn't be doing this if I were you."

Desi was right. Yes, I admit that sometimes I push too much. But what choice did I have? My schedule was tight and I wanted to make the most of it!

Desi arranged the car and Sudana drove to my hotel in the wee hours. I was ready and we hit the road early in the morning. Actually, it turned out to be a smooth drive without much traffic. The air was cool and the landscape was vibrant green all along the way. Bali gets plenty of rain and an equally warm sun soaks the place with sunshine just like any other tropical country. Trees and plants grow here throughout the year. Sudana was a jovial guy and was chatting non-stop while driving the car.

"*My type of guy,*" I thought.

He was pretty fluent in English which made my life easier. Once we crossed Sanur, Sudana suggested a coffee break.

"Yeah, why not?" I agreed although I had a cup of coffee before we left.

But hey, it doesn't do any harm to have another fresh cup of café latte in the morning. Sudana parked his car in a patio restaurant overlooking a green valley along the slope of a rolling hill just below the restaurant. The tropical flowers and the trees nestled in the rice terraces were basking in the sun. The morning haze was not totally gone and hung near the horizon, thus silhouetting the rolling hills. What a view! It was an ideal spot to sit down all day and watch as the tranquil morning slowly rolled in and then gently faded away as the sun set behind the western hills. It was the perfect morning, a perfect start to the day—serene, quiet and peaceful! We enjoyed the serenity while sipping coffee and watching time go by.

"Let's head out, otherwise we will be late," said Sudana as he finished his coffee. He was ready to move.

Besakih is not just a temple. It is a temple complex in the village of Besakih sitting on the slope of Mount Agung in Eastern Bali. It is the largest and holiest temple in Bali. The complex has three iconic Hindu Gods, Shiva the destroyer, Brahma the creator and Vishnu the preserver with the God Agung at the centre. It is a perfect blend of two cultures.

We were the first visitors to arrive at the temple. Unless a family needs to perform certain rituals, which is very common in Bali, fewer visitors show up that early in the morning. Some shops were already open, selling the offerings needed for rituals and special clothing that people often needed to wear before entering the temple. As a standard ritual, one is required to wear a 'sarong,' a printed cloth wrapped around the waist, before entering the temple complex. This is to show respect to the God and Goddess inside the temple. Sudana stayed in the car and I entered the complex on my own. The entrance had long stairs leading to the main complex. On both sides, there were displays of many Gods and demons that I was not familiar with. Certainly, the signs of a fusion between original Hindu mythology and local Balinese faith were evident. Although, I was not sure about the era when it happened. No doubt there were some differences in manifestation, but the fundamental link between the two faiths remained the same. Mainstream Hinduism has the same concepts as seen in Bali where the battle always happens between good and evil i.e. the Gods with demons.

Inside the complex, there were many shrines, but not all were accessible to the visitors. A guide approached me to take me inside, but I turned the offer down. This practice is present in most temples in India as well. I usually enjoy walking around on my own and exploring at my own pace. True, with guides one probably has better access to many shrines that are not allowed while touring alone but I was not interested in venturing inside the shrines. I was more interested in observing the architecture of the temples. While walking around, I noticed some devotees approaching one of the temple complexes. The men wore white clothes and the ladies wore colourful dresses. I was a bit curious about what was going on! Once they were inside the temple complex, I slowly approached it. I leaned against the gate and peeped inside. It appeared to be a ceremony of some kind. I was surprised to note that the rituals were similar to what I could remember from my days in India. The devotees were making offerings to God in the same manner as Hindus do in India. Perhaps it's natural that when two religions merge, some practices remain common. But I found it interesting as I did not know what to expect in such a ceremony. I was just a curious onlooker here and not a guest. A priest noticed me.

"Sir, this is a private ceremony. You cannot go in," the priest came and told me politely.

Oh my God, it didn't occur to me that it was totally inappropriate for me to watch a private ceremony. I was intruding on their privacy. What had happened to my manners? I suppose it had slipped my mind due to my curiosity. I was ashamed. I apologized profusely and left the place. I had crossed a line in my overexcitement to learn about the culture.

Since the temples were built on a slope, more temples were visible at a slightly higher elevation. I went up further to get a closer look at them. When I reached the top, I looked around. Oh my God! The view was spectacular. Green hills started not far from where the complex ended and extended for miles till where Mount Agung stood at the horizon. It was a picture-perfect morning of total serenity. I wanted to spend some more time here. But I checked my watch. Sudana had given me an hour or so. I sighed. There was no time to enjoy the beauty of nature!

On our way back to Bali, Sudana showed me typical Balinese homes on both sides of the road. To my surprise, most homes had private temples and were built on large lands. The residential part covered almost one-third of the total land and the rest was used to build the temple. There are many Gods in Hinduism. As a matter of fact, there are Gods assigned to all aspects of life. I observed that, in Balinese homes, temples are commonly dedicated to specific Gods. The more affluent a person, the bigger the temple. It was different in India where owning a temple as part of a residence was outside the reach of most common people. People normally worshipped at community temples.

Sudana explained that the rituals and prayers in each home are very much family-oriented and neighbours are not usually invited to attend the prayers. In the beginning that surprised me, as in India where I grew up, prayers and offerings in shrines were a community affair. So these prayers offered in the seclusion of the home baffled me. Later, I slowly began to understand the concept. Actually, such prayers and offerings are almost a daily affair in most Balinese homes, so no gatherings are needed.

I asked Sudana, "Is it possible to visit a Balinese home?"

He thought for a moment and said, "Ok, I can take you to a home that is open to visitors if you are interested. But it will delay your return to Bali. I have strict instructions from Desi to bring you back on time."

I laughed. Desi was protecting my interests and schedules like a mother hen. Atta girl! My trusted tour organizer for sure. She knew very well that I had a habit of pushing things.

"No worries, I will be quick," I assured Sudana.

I wanted to visit at least one Balinese home to get a vibe of their lifestyle. Sudana took me to a home that was open to visitors. There were many temples inside the housing complex as he had explained earlier. As with the other homes, each temple was devoted to one of the many Hindu Gods. However, I found one temple that was dedicated only to the deceased ones in the family. When asked, Sudana told me that this practice was common to all Balinese homes. I found this quite interesting. This was, once again, a manifestation of how often rituals get blended with local traditions and beliefs and this was how religious practices transformed to a new dimension after migration.

But all good times come to an end and it was time to return to Bali. Otherwise 'Missy' Desi would be upset and tell me off for getting late for my next venture. Nevertheless, it was indeed a wonderful morning. I spent time with Sudana and learned about Balinese culture. Fortunately, the traffic was light on our way back and I was on time for my paragliding adventure. Sudana too was relieved about arriving on time. He was in no mood to face the wrath of my wonderful tour organizer.

I didn't have to wait long and the jeep from the paragliding club came to pick me up from the hotel. We travelled through the outskirts of Bali to Pandwa beach. There were other thrill seekers like me waiting there to paraglide. This was not my first time with this sport. I enjoyed paragliding in Malaysia and Vietnam. In Hanoi, my programme almost got cancelled due to extreme fog. But here, it was quite the opposite! It was sunny and the afternoon was warm with very little breeze, ideal weather for paragliding.

"Can I do it on my own?" I asked Ketut, my instructor. It would have been good to do it solo.

"No Sir, we don't allow visitors to jump solo," he replied in a matter-of-fact voice.

I realized that there was no point arguing with him. And he was right, it becomes a liability issue if someone gets into an accident. You never know, just a slight shift in the wind and one could easily be adrift over the Indian Ocean if one doesn't control the parachute well.

Nevertheless, I was excited. When my turn came, the crew fixed my harness and we took off from a cliff next to the Indian Ocean. Once airborne, I looked around. Wow, it was beautiful! The turquoise-blue ocean met the sky at the distant horizon. Waves were continuously breaking on the shore spreading white foam.

"*Yeah, it's time to do some photography,*" I thought and pressed the button of my GoPro video camera fastened to my chest harness.

Damn! The button was stuck. I tried again but no luck. I should have tested it before taking off. Although I was wearing sunglasses with a built-in video camera, another set of lenses with a higher resolution would have been handy. It was my GoPro that I was counting on for that.

"Are you okay there?" Ketut asked me, hovering over my shoulder. He had felt that I was struggling with something.

"Yeah, my camera doesn't work. I need a camera. Can we abort?"

"What kind of camera?" I could hardly hear him due to the wind.

"GoPro."

"Ok, we will pick one up from my stock. There is a bit of a rental charge though."

Ketut didn't make any fuss about aborting the flight. I must say it was really nice of him to abort a flight in midair just for a camera! In a way it was good that we took the flight in tandem, otherwise, I would have regretted flying solo without my video camera! So, we touched down quickly to borrow a GoPro and soon we were airborne again! I was a happy camper. Both my video cameras were running and capturing the world around me. I just relaxed and enjoyed watching the beauty of the endless ocean as far as I could see. I was mesmerized by the view of the vast ocean stretching up to the horizon with ripples in turquoise-blue water shining in the bright afternoon sun. We made a semi-circle over Pandwa beach. The white sandy beach was glowing in the bright sunlight! We flew over the ocean and made a wide turn towards the dunes near the beach. The twenty minutes of flying time was worth every penny.

My evening was free and that suited me just fine. I ventured to a local restaurant to try some more Nasi Goreng... well, a mild version actually.

This was my second try with Nasi Goreng. Unless one warns the waiter while placing the order, one can be surprised by how hot it can be. I love good food, but I'm careful about the spices and chilly, especially while travelling. As all my events were scheduled back-to-back, I couldn't afford to be sick. Most spicy foods taste great, but I didn't have a choice here. Strict travel rules! So far, the routine had worked well in all my journeys and I had no regrets.

It's a cool place!

The next day was packed with water sports. I am usually not keen on them but it was Desi's idea. Actually, that was an understatement. I couldn't even swim! Due to my fear of drowning, I had never been comfortable in water but Desi was persistent.

"My friend, when you come to Bali, you have to do some water sports. Everyone does it."

"Listen dear, I am not a water sports kind of guy."

"Why not? They are fun."

"Desi, I know they are fun but I don't even know to swim," I confessed.

Desi giggled over the phone, "Oh my God, you don't know how to swim and you are coming to Bali? How will you survive here?"

"That's exactly what I am trying to tell you. I just want to survive," I chuckled over the phone.

But Desi wouldn't budge and persisted, "You wouldn't die, my friend. I wouldn't let that happen."

Besides, that was the kind of package she arranged for her clients. She first booked me for two sports—snorkelling and walking on the sea bed. Then she tried to convince me with a third one.

"Have you done waterboarding before?" she began.

"What on earth is that?"

"You are lifted in the air by the force of a water jet."

"*Oh, no… not for me,*" I thought and almost snapped at her. "I will skip it, Desi. I told you I don't know how to swim."

Desi snapped back, "Why not? It is a lot of fun! There is no danger to it."

"Listen, anything above the ground is fine with me, but not with water sports."

She chuckled, "Don't chicken out!"

"I'm serious. Would you do it if I ask you to join?"

"Hey, you are a tourist, I'm not. So, calm down," she said and wouldn't let it go, "No worries, the instructor will work with you in tandem. Do it first and then tell me whether you like it or not."

I gave up with a sigh. So Desi booked me into three water sports. But none of the sports included parasailing which would have been more interesting for me. Actually, I had some experience of parasailing and I liked it. It was a cool game and similar to paragliding, but over water and that was fun. Unless there is a crisis, it doesn't require swimming.

So I nagged Desi, "Hey, what happened to my parasailing?"

"You have already booked for paragliding on the previous day. Do you want to go parasailing too?"

"Yes Desi, these are two different sports altogether."

I could hear her sigh over the phone. Anyway, she booked me for parasailing too. Finally, it was done and I was relieved. To be honest, parasailing was my favourite. Actually, I think it is safer than paragliding. The risk of drifting away in parasailing is almost none as one is tied to the boat with a toe-line. To me, it is relaxing. The landing is also interesting—one just skims over the surface of the water to reduce the momentum and then lands on a deck or the beach. Unlike parasailing, paragliding requires a high mountain or a cliff to jump off. Parasailing is only possible over a water body and Bali has quite a few of those! So, I was not going to miss this chance of parasailing over the Indian Ocean and counted on Desi for fixing me up for this, and she did.

Fortunately, Tanjung Benoa beach was a convenient ten minutes drive from my hotel in Nusa Dua.

"Go to the office and register please," the driver told me.

"*Wow! Pretty formal, I guess,*" I thought.

The office was nothing but a shack with some small desks on the beach.

I told the guy at the front desk, "Let's start with my favourite one, parasailing."

"You are booked for fifteen minutes of airtime, Sir," the guy told me flatly.

"Are you kidding? You don't even settle in the air in fifteen minutes! What are you talking about?" I snapped back.

"Fifteen minutes, Sir, that's the deal you paid for."

Bloody hell! I had not discussed the details with Desi. This was totally my fault. Now I was busted. But I was not ready to give up so fast.

"Ok, what are your charges for half an hour? Let's be reasonable," I said as I started bargaining.

"Double of what you paid, Sir," said the guy as he started checking his list, probably trying to find out how much I had paid.

"Hey listen! I paid for four water sports altogether. Give me a good deal, will you?"

The guy was shaking his head while looking for my booking. After a little more haggling, it seemed to work out. I bargained and after reducing the rate, we settled for thirty minutes of flying time. I patted my back.

It was showtime! Once the harness connected, I made a run on the sandy beach. It was a short run, just for a few seconds. The chute opened right away. The wind was strong and bingo! The drag pulled me up from the ground and raised me high above. Yay, I was airborne. Ah, heaven! I flew over the ocean and looked around. The view from the sky was out of this world. Other than some occasional rustling of the wind, there was total silence around me. I loved it! The world was so peaceful! I was swaying and drifting in the wind, the boats sailing far below were dots over the vast ocean.

I loved it so much that I didn't want to touch down on the beach again. But all good times must come to an end. The thirty minutes of air time passed by just like that. It was a smooth touchdown. Fortunately, my video camera did not trouble me this time. I quickly checked some video clips. When I got back home, these clips would be my treasure! Anyway, they looked fine. The only downside was that the camera had somehow reset to its factory setting and the time stamping was wrong. Ah well, it was not a big deal! I could live with that.

"Are you ready?" the same guy came up to me and asked. I hardly had a chance to catch my breath after touchdown.

"Ready for what?"

"We are going snorkelling in five minutes," he said, grinning from ear to ear.

"Five minutes?" I said aloud and thought, "*Bloody hell! I just started to relax a bit.*"

"Yes, five minutes. Put on your life vest. I will come and pick you up in five minutes."

"*Gee, these guys mean business,*" I thought and asked him, "Wait. Where are we heading to?"

He pointed to a boat anchored nearby and left. I had not had much luck with snorkelling earlier. Let me rewind a bit. My first experience in Phuket, Thailand, was a disaster. I practically drowned when I tried to float in the sea. Shawn, my Australian guide in Phuket, who was in the water helping others with snorkelling realized my problem and yelled, "Go to the boat and wear double vests. It will give you some extra float."

So I somehow went back huffing and puffing to the boat and doubled my vest. That didn't help, it gave me too much of float. I lost control and started drifting away. At that point, Shawn realized that I was worse than a newbie! So he left the others and came to my rescue with a rubber tube. He asked me to hang from one end of the rubber tube while he held the other. He then dragged me into the water and swam around holding the rubber tube while I tried to snorkel. Needless to say, that didn't go well either. It was a mess!

Was I embarrassed? Not really. I enjoyed piggybacking and loved the sight of coral reefs on the seabed (or the limited amount that I could see).

"What a shameless character," my wife taunted me later.

I couldn't care less and tried snorkelling again in Costa Rica, on the Pacific coast a few years later. Disaster struck again! I panicked and almost drowned, taking the crew with me. Oh yes, it was quite a show under the water. Anyway, that's a story for another day! My friends advised me to take more swimming lessons before heading to Bali. So I did. I gained a teeny-weeny bit of confidence from them but was not very successful. Well, I mostly splashed water. One cannot call that swimming. But I think the lessons helped.

In Bali, a guide stayed close to me all the time because he knew my challenges. But I must say I did a fair job this time.

"*Not bad, not bad at all*," I thought as I gave him a thumbs up.

Oh boy, it sure was fun! Unlike my time in Phuket, when I suffered from anxiety all the time when in water, I thoroughly enjoyed the corals under the sea this time. This success gave me the confidence that I needed when later I snorkelled in the Java Sea during my trip to Komodo island from Bali.

The crew pulled my ladder up once I was done with snorkelling. I took my gear off and was about to take the towel out from my backpack to dry myself when the guide walked in behind me.

He grinned and said, "Not so fast, my friend!"

I turned around and looked at him. I wasn't sure what he meant!

"Get ready for the next game," he continued.

"What next game?"

"You are going back into the water again. This time to walk on the sea bed," he grinned as if he was enjoying my misery.

Oh crap! In my excitement, I had totally forgotten about that. I had paid for four games altogether, and this was one of them. I had never done it before and I was not sure how it was going to turn out.

"*Not fair, it was time to relish my hard-earned confidence from a few minutes ago*," I thought.

Suddenly the anxiety of facing another challenge under the water threw a black cloud over my jubilant mood.

"*Damn!*" I thought.

All my euphoria vaporized instantly and I tried to play the sympathy card, "You know, eh? I told you before that I don't know how to swim."

"I know. No worries, you are not going to swim this time."

"Yeah, I realize that. Will there be a guide with me then?"

"No, not with you. But close by," the guy assured me while fixing the harness on me.

"*That's no good. How am I going to survive down there alone?*" I thought and began to worry.

The guy must have read my mind. He grinned again and continued to work with his gear. He seemed to find my constant anxiety and miserable state of mind funny.

"*Oh, what the hell,*" I thought, stayed quiet and decided to go with the flow.

First, he placed a helmet on me. It was a special air-tight helmet. The helmet had a latch under the chin to seal any air gap. It looked like the helmets that astronauts wear. I felt like a total zombie with it covering my head and face! There was a long tube connected from the back of the helmet to a large oxygen tank installed near the stairwell. He tied a chord to my waistband once the helmet was in place. He checked everything all around and when he was satisfied, he came to the front and pulled the helmet from my head so that I could pay attention to his instructions.

"With the oxygen tube hooked up to the tank on the boat, you won't have any breathing trouble."

"*To be honest, I am not really convinced,*" I told myself silently.

Also, I would have been more comfortable with an oxygen tank on my back rather than it being on a boat far away from me.

"So that is my lifeline?"

"Yeah, part of it. The chord is the other part."

"What happens if that snaps?" I asked as I wanted to make sure that I was totally safe.

But the guy ignored my query and said, "You wouldn't die. We are here. Now listen carefully. Climb down the ladder into the water. Let yourself sink slowly."

"Aha, the guy doesn't know that I sink like a rock," I thought to myself.

I sink like a brick all the time, no matter how hard I try to float. Anyway, I listened to him patiently.

"The chord will be connected to the boat and we will watch it. There is a life vest fastened to you for safety."

I knew from my experience that one life vest wouldn't be good enough for me. That's fine, there was no point arguing about the vest.

"It is what it is," I thought.

He showed me a button near the waistband and instructed, "When you are done, press the button, and we will slowly pull the rope."

"Aha, the button would be my life saver…" I mused quietly.

I affectionately played my fingers over the button. Yes, it was better to make sure I knew where it was. I did not know when I might need it.

"What happens if the chord gets tangled?" I wanted to discuss everything that could go wrong.

"Ah, why are you getting so nervous? One of us will be around close by and we will pull you up. No worries. Besides, there is a metal rail down there. Hold on to that for balance."

Ah, that gave me some confidence.

"Not a bad idea for a newbie like me," I thought.

I didn't want to make another ruckus as I had in Costa Rica where I had tried to grab someone's leg in a desperate attempt to survive while trying to snorkel.

"Walk around down there for half an hour. Look at the coral reef and enjoy the scenery around you. We will pull you up once you are done," said the guide as he looked at his watch.

He probably could not wait all day long to answer all my questions. He had other clients to take care of. He placed the air-tight helmet on my head and latched it. I was cut off from the outside world. Another guy came down carrying an underwater camera that I had rented from them. No, I was not going to fiddle with the camera underwater when my main focus was just to survive against all odds! I asked him to carry it.

Was I nervous? Of course, I was very nervous. First of all, water sports make me tense. I feel comfortable with any sports played above ground level. The world of water is not my cup of tea. Secondly, I had no idea how far away the other person would be if I needed help. I wouldn't be able to scream even if I needed to. My only lifesaver was the SOS button on my waistband which could be used to call for help. That said, I was feeling the adrenaline rush already.

"*After all, it was not swimming. It was just walking on the sea bed,*" I assured myself.

As I said, I had never done it before, so I was nervous. But I was excited too. I knew that with the oxygen tank connected to my helmet, I wouldn't have to struggle for air while hopping around under water. I could always come up to the surface holding the metal rail if I needed to. With all these things in my favour, how difficult would it be to just walk down there for a few minutes?

"*No big deal,*" I told myself.

I felt a bit relieved and finally, I was game! The guide showed me a V-sign and waved me off the ladder. Once I climbed down the last step of the ladder, I looked up. I saw the guide above me, following me down the ladder.

"*Ok then, nothing to worry about,*" I told myself and lowered myself into the water.

Bloody hell, the same problem happened again! The buoyancy of the water made me feel weightless and I lost control. I held on to the metal rail of the ladder tightly. The sea bed was not too far down from where the ladder ended, perhaps fifteen feet below. I took a deep breath and let go. Somehow I managed to lower myself onto the sea bed while trying to control my float.

I then stood up and tried to walk. I was not stable. I was hopping rather than walking. I saw something close by, a refracted image of something like a metal rail standing on the sea bed. The light was dim and I squinted. I was right. It was a metal handrail installed on the sea bed. I gave myself a push to reach it and grabbed the rail. I started hopping just like a person walking on the moon. Soon I was close to a coral reef, similar to the ones I had seen earlier while snorkelling. I went closer and a bunch of fish swam away. They were close enough to grab. I was feeling confident at that point.

Usually, I find breathing underwater very difficult as I gasp for air in a panic. With the oxygen line connected to the air-tight helmet, that fear factor was now completely gone. I started enjoying my new sport. I came to the end of the rail and daringly swam towards the coral reef. At that point, I got used to the lightness of my body and the dim light around me. I also knew that I was connected to the boat with a rope. So I had no fear of drowning either. Oh God, people in this world make the entertainment industry idiot-proof for the people like me! I swam from one coral reef to another, trying to touch the colourful fish swarming around me. I enjoyed every moment of it!

I became a little child as I swam and hopped from one coral reef to another in the dim light of the ocean. I witnessed a completely different world. I had never experienced such a delight before. Time passed by just like that! I didn't even realize when the half-hour finished. I saw the guide from a nearby coral reef (pretty much a shadowy figure in dim light) signalling me to move towards the ladder. It was time! Suddenly, sadness crept over me as I prepared to leave the wonderful world of natural beauty all around me. But I knew that it was time to go. With a sigh, I moved back to grab the handrail to reach the bottom of the ladder. Once up, the guide helped me take off my gear. He was obviously happy to see me climbing up in one piece!

"Did you enjoy the walk, Sir?"

"Can I go for one more round?" I replied with a smile.

"Perhaps another time. You still need to go for another water sport, Sir!"

"*Oh no, never-ending water sports, why on earth did I allow Desi to book me so many?*" I thought as I checked my watch.

He was right. Three done, one more to go.

I shrugged, "Ok, then, let's head out."

The boat was already moving towards the shoreline. I pulled out the towel from my backpack and dried myself. I didn't have to. The breeze from the ocean was good enough.

Once back on the beach, I found that the place was swarming with people. Thrill seekers from all over the world came here to have some fun. Bali is, indeed, a paradise for various water sports which are part of the big tourism industry here. The Indian Ocean here is very calm and relatively shallow which is ideal for water sports even for newbies. While waiting for the crew to arrive for my next venture, I watched tourists of all age groups having fun with several water sports. Suddenly a newlywed Indian couple caught my attention. I was pretty sure they had come here to spend their honeymoon. The couple was trying to manoeuvre a water taxi, commonly known here as a 'water scooter.' It must have been their first try because I could hear all kinds of expressions such as 'Wow', 'Oh My God', 'No way I'm going to do it', 'Are you crazy?' etc. as they tried their level best. Suddenly the scooter fell sideways into the water and the air was filled with their screams and laughter. It was hilarious to watch them having fun! No wonder, Bali is a desired destination for many honeymooning couples.

"Come to this side, Sir," said a voice.

I turned around and looked up at the guy who was calling me. He was my new instructor. Most likely he was assigned for my last water event to complete my miserable cycle. (Well, I exaggerate. It hadn't been that bad so far).

"Wear this helmet please," he continued. "Do you want a guide to go with you or do you want to go solo?" he asked while fixing the helmet on my head.

I had no idea what kind of sport waterboarding was and what were the risks involved.

"Ha? Do I need a guide?" I asked him while he fastened the water exhaust around my waist.

"It's up to you, Sir. Some do and some don't. It's your call, Sir."

Then looking at my hopeless face, he softened a bit and asked, "Have you done waterboarding before?"

"Never. I don't have a clue what it is."

"Perhaps it is not a bad idea to take a guide for the first time, Sir. You would need to balance yourself when up in the air."

I thought about his suggestion for a moment, "*Well, if I cannot balance myself, it will definitely be a plunge into the swirling whirlpool below. What's the downside? Hmm, then I will be forced to practice my half-assed swimming lesson in trying to survive. Not a chance.*"

"Yeah, I will go in tandem," I told him.

"Very well, Sir, I will call you when we are ready."

The guide left me there to wait. I had all my gear on and that made me look like an alien from outer space.

"*Oh well, when in Rome, do as the Romans do,*" I told myself and relaxed.

But I didn't have to wait for long. Soon, the guide came back with another person.

He introduced him, "He will be your guide and he will take it from here."

"*Very well! A change of guard,*" I thought.

"Come with me, Sir," said the new guide and started walking in front of me.

I followed him to the shoreline from where he boarded a water scooter and was ready to go. The guy sat in the driver's seat and asked me to sit in the back.

"*Oh, no... deep sea again,*" I thought as my stress level rose in anticipation as I feared the unknown adventure.

"Where to?" I asked.

"We will take you to the deep part of the ocean where we have the water pump."

I mentally cringed, "*Oh, crap!*" and asked him, "Can you explain what this sport is all about?"

"Simple. We hook you up to the water jet and you go up in the air," he said in a businesslike manner while starting the scooter.

It was late in the afternoon, but the beach was still bursting with activity. Tourists were busy with all kinds of water sports and guides were running around to help them. To them, I was just one of many clients. The guide hardly had any time for chit-chat. He just wanted to complete his assignment and chase a new client. He started the scooter and took off with a big splash which sprayed water all over me. It was the first time I was riding a water scooter and I must say that was part of the fun. I used to ride motorcycles during my early days and had always enjoyed it. Within a few minutes, he pulled the scooter next to a platform anchored to the sea bed below. A large water pump occupied one side of the platform. Once we reached the platform, the guide unfastened my water intake hose from my waistband and fitted it under my feet. Then he gently lowered me into the water. To be honest, I could not have reached the water on my own without his help. I couldn't even walk with my gear fitted under my feet nor was I capable of any natural movement, other than perhaps crawling. While I was floating in the water wearing my life vest, my guide fastened his harness to my waistline and held me upright. Another guy dragged the other end of the water intake hose connected to the bottom of my feet and hooked it to a water pump with the hose tucked awkwardly under my feet. At that moment, I was totally immobile with the hose dangling from my feet. I was just trying to keep my balance. The next moment, a big thrust from the water jet under my feet suddenly pushed me upwards and made me airborne. Damn! With the sudden thrust, I totally lost my balance and was about to topple. The guide who was also pushed upwards with me held on to me tightly and yanked me to keep me upright. I am sure he had handled many newbies like me and knew this game very well. Anyway, I struggled to keep my balance with the constant thrust from the water pump keeping me high up in the air.

"Stand straight," he shouted from behind.

In a minute or so I managed to find my balance and I could stand straight up in the air at a height of 15-20 feet while counterbalancing the water jet below.

"*Hey, not so bad, not bad at all!*" I told myself.

I felt the adrenaline rush in my body and was thrilled with my newly-found confidence. Suddenly the thrust which was controlled by the pump below was gone and I fell from the height right away like a stone. Wow, I felt butterflies in my stomach as I fell! A moment before I hit the water, the jet pushed me up again and I needed to balance once more against the thrust. Yahoo! Actually, I was getting the hang of it and had started to balance myself pretty well. The game went on with the water jet pushing me up and down for about 10 minutes. To tell you the truth, I enjoyed every moment of it. Then came the final moment of the game and the thrust was reduced to a slower rate so that we could touch down on the water smoothly.

"Wow! What an experience!" I thought.

I was over the moon. I crawled back onto the platform and someone helped me untie my gear so that I could walk again!

"Thank God," I thought as I felt human again!

I thanked my guide and we boarded the scooter and returned to the beach. Finally, it was the end of my water sports! In a way, I felt relieved. It was time to collect my stuff and head out. No, I did not bring a checklist of what I wanted to do in Bali. I am a thrill seeker and I always try to find some fun when I travel to different places. This adventure surely made my day! Later, I thanked Desi for arranging these thrilling sports for me. I didn't even know that they existed. Oh yeah, I remembered to ask for the memory card containing the images. Years down the road, those images would be my treasure!

I checked my watch. It was around 4:00 pm. The tour company gave me a ride back to my hotel. The sun was slowly moving towards the horizon and the long shadows of the trees by the roadside were quietly signalling the end of a beautiful day. Desi and Kadek were to pick me up from the hotel at around 5 pm for dinner. So I hardly had enough time to freshen up. Desi suggested that we drive to town to grab our dinner. I was fine with the idea. A quick shower in the hotel made me feel much better. Suddenly I realized that I didn't have my glasses with me. These were my prescription glasses and I needed them, especially when it was dark. I searched my room thoroughly but couldn't trace them. I tried to recollect where I had last seen them.

"I must have left it in the locker room at the beach," I told myself.

I phoned the tour company and they assured me that they would give me a call as soon as they found out, but that did not happen.

"I lost my glasses," I told Desi and Kadek when I met them in the lobby.

"Really? Where?" she asked me.

"I don't recall exactly, perhaps in the locker room at the beach."

Desi tried to call them but no one picked up. It was already quite late so I was not surprised. Fortunately, I had a copy of the prescription in my backpack. I generally carry one to be on the safe side.

"Let's go into town. I know an optician," Desi told me and we headed out.

Desi talked to the optician and gave him my prescription while I waited.

The gentleman looked at it and said apologetically, "We cannot get it done here. We have to send it to Jakarta and it will take a few days.

Well, I didn't have a few days to spare. I was leaving Bali in a couple of days.

"Forget the glasses, I will manage. Let's go and eat," I told Desi.

Since I was not driving myself, I could manage without it.

"Ok then, let's try the food court here. It's a decent place with plenty of choices," said Kadek.

"Sure, I am fine with that."

Kadek parked the car and we headed towards the food court. Guess what? It was Nasi Goreng again! It looks like my fate was sealed in Indonesia. This dish was everywhere!

"That's it! I'm not going to eat any more Nasi Goreng during my trip," I told Desi and she laughed.

I was a bit upset about losing my glasses. But Desi and Kadek made it a fun evening for me. They gave me company and we passed a pleasant evening chatting and joking together. I needed that. They were both easygoing and fun-loving people. We strolled for a while after dinner. I just wanted to get a feel of the place.

"Is it downtown? Well, is it commonly known here as downtown?" I asked.

"Of course! This is the business part of the town and I cross it every day while going to work," Desi told me.

"Not a bad setup," I reflected.

I checked my watch. It was getting a bit late. The next day would be my last day in Bali and it was going to be a hectic one. Although I was done with the sun-soaked beaches, I intended to explore the heartland of Bali and its culture with Desi tagging along with me.

"Let's go back to the hotel. I have to be up in the morning," I said.

"I know, I know! I will be coming with you too," laughed Desi.

The girl was always so cheerful and that made a difference! The car park was close by. It was Sunday, but the traffic was still horrendous, especially in the downtown. Then it suddenly happened! An accident involving our car! A lady riding a motorcycle with a girl sitting in the back seat swerved from the right and cut in front of our car. Bang! Both riders fell after hitting our car. The motorcycle skidded on the road and the wheels were still turning! Clearly, it was the lady's fault. We had just been crawling in the traffic when she cut us off. A traffic cop was close by and he came right away.

"*OMG, what next?*" I wondered.

I am used to a standard process when an accident happens in North America. The ambulance and the fire truck arrive right away, the police investigate the accident and issue a ticket to the faulty driver. But not in Bali! A crowd surrounded the scene right away and helped the lady get onto the motorcycle again. Fortunately, since we were crawling in the traffic, neither the lady nor the girl riding with her was badly hurt. Nonetheless, they were visibly shaken. Surprisingly, there was hardly any damage to our car. The impact was minor probably due to our slow speed. The police waved us off. To the cop, traffic control on a busy road was more important than issuing a ticket. He wanted to clear the mess and didn't want another jam on the road.

"Move, move," he said as he gestured for us to get out of there and we were happy to leave.

What a relief! I hope the lady learned a lesson from the accident, especially since she was riding with the girl, possibly her daughter. Her passenger was not wearing a helmet. I certainly hoped this was a wake-up call for her. Anyway, it was close to 11 pm when Kadek and Desi dropped me at the hotel. We all were a bit shaken by the accident, it could have been worse. Two lives had been in mortal danger and no matter whose fault it was, we had been involved. It was a close call! No, I didn't want to think about it any further and called it a night!

Bali, a place rich in cultural heritage

Have you ever woken up in a dark room and couldn't figure out where you were? You may have felt confused and somewhat lost. This might have happened to some of you. Well, that's what I felt like when I woke up in my hotel room in Bali. My curtains were drawn, so the room was dark. The air conditioner was humming monotonously. I looked around, half asleep and couldn't figure out where I was in the semi-darkness.

"Where am I? This doesn't look like my bed in Calgary!" I reflected.

I checked the time on my watch. It was almost 5 am. Ok, I usually wake up around this time. I listened carefully. I could hear the birds chirping outside. They didn't sound familiar and this confused me further. Suddenly, it struck me that I was travelling and this was my hotel in Bali. I almost jumped out of bed! Then I remembered that the rental car was coming to pick me up at 8 am, so there was no rush as such. What a relief! I relaxed and cosily wrapped the blanket around me to get some more sleep. No such luck. Tossing and turning in bed didn't help. My sleep had simply slipped away. While lying under the blanket, I recollected that it was my last day in Bali. The last two days had been hectic, mainly to fulfil my thirst for adventures. But there was plenty to do in Bali itself to get a vibe of the place and its cultural heritage.

I sighed as I realized that I had to leave Bali the next day. Sadness was slowly creeping within me. I had fallen in love with the place. Though I had been there only for two days, it seemed like I had been here for ages. How long had I known Desi and Kadek? Not for long. But it seemed like I had known them forever and they were a part of me.

On my last day here, I kept the whole day aside only to explore Bali, nothing else—no beaches, no water sports, and no monkey business in the sky. Just to know Bali in its entirety before I left and to learn about the place where Hindu mythology had left its footprints hundreds of years ago. That was the real Bali and I couldn't leave without knowing her heritage. Desi would tag along with me all day. It was not easy to convince her to come on board. I had to twist her arm a little. I learned that she loves ice cream. So I dangled the carrot in front of her.

"I will buy you as much ice cream as you want."

I was hoping that she would fall for the bait and she did!

"Promise?" she asked.

"Promise," I concurred.

She grinned with a beautiful, innocent smile. I laughed as I lay on the bed, remembering our conversation as we made the deal.

But lying down was not an option. There was plenty to do in the morning. I indulged myself by taking a long hot shower and then headed down for breakfast. I had a nice and leisurely breakfast while sitting on the outdoor patio and enjoyed every moment of it. There were very few tourists at that early hour and the morning was serene and peaceful. The birds were chirping from the trees nearby and jumping from one branch to another. Some sparrows from a nearby guava tree were waiting for the right moment when they could dive into my plate. Getting a piece of omelette early in the morning was definitely a bonus for them. I obliged them a little. After all, I was on holiday and the birds were entitled to share some of my goodies as well.

"Sir, your car has arrived," said the waitress, while holding out the coffee.

Already? I checked my watch. Wow! Sudana was there at 8 am sharp. I guess he was getting the hang of my travel habits. While enjoying my breakfast with the sparrows, I seemed to have lost track of time. Although another cup of coffee was very tempting at that moment, it would be unfair to keep Sudana waiting for me in the lobby. I thanked the waitress and headed for the lobby.

"Hurry up… there is a lot of traffic on the road," he said.

"Relax my friend, we will make it."

"No boss, the traffic is a bit more than usual today."

"Ok, ok… off we go! Give me five minutes to go get my backpack."

Saying this, I rushed to my room. When I came back, Sudana had already left the lobby to start the car. I jumped into the SUV and he rolled the beast right away. It was Monday rush hour. So yes, there was some traffic on the road but it was flowing regularly and at a decent pace, not jammed chock-a-bloc. We crossed Sanur and headed towards Batubulan. That was the plan. We first had to pick up Desi near her home in Batubulan. It's further north of Sanur. She was ready and jumped into the car as soon as we stopped. We then headed out. The plan was to first attend a village play called Barong Dance near Sanur. It was Desi's idea. When I booked the trip, I told her that I would like to get a taste of the Balinese culture and heritage. She was the one who suggested the Barong Dance, a traditional village play. When we reached the village, she asked me to wait outside.

"Hey, don't go alone… I will buy the ticket," I said as I tried to stop her.

All expenses were mine. That was the deal.

"Shhh," she said and gestured for me to be quiet and left for the ticket counter. When she returned, she had two tickets in her hand. With a big smile, she said, "Half price, Sir."

Desi had managed to get two tickets at a discounted rate. Wow! I couldn't have done it if I had been alone. She was able to since she was a local. Hey, my investment in ice cream was already paying off! We walked inside. It was a small open-air theatre with a gallery-type seating arrangement. Soon, the place filled up with tourists, mostly foreigners. I was sitting with Desi near the front row. While we waited for the play to start, she briefed me about it.

"This is how it goes. The Barong Dance represents the eternal struggle between good and evil spirits. They are all mythological characters. Barong is a mythological animal and represents a good spirit, whereas Rangda is a mythological monster that represents an evil spirit."

I interrupted, "You know Desi, a similar concept also exists in India. We burn effigies of the bad spirits in India during certain festivals."

"You may be right! This is true in many of our festivals… Shhh! It's starting!"

We quietened. During the entire play lasting one hour, various characters appeared on the stage and transformed themselves into fearsome animals threatening the good spirit. The play actually ended with fights between good and evil, just to reflect the eternal struggle which never ends between the epic dichotomies of human life. I tried to absorb as much as I could as they were speaking in Bahasa and my knowledge of the language was very limited. Desi was explaining things to me from time to time. As a matter of fact, I was thankful that she was with me. It always helps to have a local person who can explain the details during such an event. The play surprised me as the Balinese culture has a lot in common with Hindu myths and Gods. One of the main characters of the play was Dewi (Devi) Kunti, a renowned figure from the Indian epic Mahabharata. Lord Siwa (Siva) in the play was another deity from the Hindu religion and the whole episode sounded familiar as if I was watching a play in an Indian village. Epics from the Hindu religion seemed to have blended here with local culture and belief. This was a perfect example of a fusion between the two cultures. When the play was over, we had a quick photo-op with the actors and actresses in the play.

"Where to now?"

"Ubud, Mas village," Desi replied while settling into the car.

I had a general idea about Ubud, but I was not aware of Mas village.

"What about it?" I asked.

"Well, you wanted to see some Balinese artwork, right? That is the place."

Of course, I realised that I had mentioned my interest to Desi although I was not sure where I would find it in Ubud.

I already knew that Bali had become a fast-growing expat haven… many people were opening small-scale businesses making bamboo handicrafts, wooden carvings and statues, paintings and many more. Not far from Sanur, Mas village in Ubud is a very peaceful place, conducive to the growth of business for both foreigners and locals alike and businesses were thriving. I could probably spend hours there watching the artists chiselling wood to create amazing handicrafts. The same goes for the paintings in Ubud. Large paintings available for sale were displayed all over the walls in spacious showrooms. Some could be pricey, but they were classy too.

We hopped from store to store, sometimes visiting the studios where artists were busy with their work. Some stores were massive, with large paintings hanging from the wall, ready for sale. Obviously, there must be buyers, otherwise these stores wouldn't be displaying paintings just to showcase Ubud's artistic culture. Desi and I could have spent some more time checking out other stores, but it was noon already and I was getting hungry.

"Let's go for a bite," I said while rubbing my tummy.

"Yeah, let's do that! I am hungry too," Desi chuckled. "Bebek Joni is a popular place for lunch among foreigners. I would prefer that, do you wanna try it?" she asked.

"Hey, as long as there is good food," I shrugged.

The place was not far from where we were. Desi had planned it well. As such, Ubud was a small town surrounded by rice fields and rice terraces. Bebek Joni was slightly away from the town. When we reached there, I was a bit surprised to find that the place swarmed with foreigners. We just walked in as we didn't have a reservation and we were lucky to get a table! The sweeping view of the vast rice fields just outside the patio is one reason that makes this place different from the others. Another good reason for its popularity was good food with plenty of choices. I settled for some good old pasta.

Yes, I know what you all are thinking. Am I crazy to try Italian food when in Bali? Well, not quite though. It was a fusion with the Indonesian recipe. Believe it or not, I found this to be true in most countries that I had travelled to. Food from another country often turns into local cuisine once it is blended with spices and herbs from that region and it plays well with the locals and tourists alike. At Bebek Joni, the food was delicious and was a well-deserved change from my usual Nasi Goreng. But guess what? Someone went crazy there in the ice cream parlour! My, oh my, the girl probably could have consumed an entire load of ice cream there.

"How can you eat so much ice cream, Desi?" I asked.

"Well, you know my weakness!" She gave me a wicked smile with a mouthful of ice cream.

Time flies when you chat! But we were getting late and there was plenty to cover in our itinerary. So we headed out right after lunch to visit other parts of Ubud which were dotted with temples. I found the Bali temples unique. Each temple is an archaeological marvel. The stone carving at the entrance of the Elephant Cave (or Goa Gajah as the locals call it) was intricate but beautiful. The temple was built in the 9th century and the site is now included in the UNESCO World Heritage list.

Pura Tirta Empul in Tampaksiring was another must-see on the list. The temple had a bathing facility where many Balinese take baths for purification. As a matter of fact, I saw many Westerners also taking baths in the holy water. As in the Besakih Temple, one is required to wear a 'sarong' before entering any of the temples. That is the custom.

Once again it struck me that the Balinese devotion to some of the Gods was similar to other Gods worshipped in India. Brahma, Visnu, and Maheswara or Siva, this Great Hindu trinity of supreme divinity was omnipresent in many of the shrines that I visited in Bali. This is one thing I also observed in Yogyakarta which I will talk about later. Talking about Hinduism, I read a few articles about when and how Hinduism had migrated to Bali. I was surprised to learn that Bali was not the first place where Hinduism had first evolved in Indonesia. It had started in Kalimantan in southern Borneo on the West Coast of Indonesia! This was quite a stretch actually! I still cannot fathom how Hinduism landed in a fairly tribal area with dense wilderness spread over miles. Perhaps the proximity of Borneo to Thailand and Cambodia where footprints of Hinduism were already present, was the catalyst. Whatever the reason may be, it continues to amaze me how an ancient religion was transported to different parts of the world thousands of miles away from India. Recently, I was in Chile in South America. I saw an active Hindu temple in Punta Arenas which is the tip of the Southern Hemisphere! In Indonesia, the language may be different and the lifestyle may have blended with the local norms, but the trail of the original Hindu religion remains the same. Indeed, many of the rituals have been transformed to blend with local practices.

The sun was going down on the horizon and dark clouds were rolling in. We were yet to visit the famous rice terraces in Ubud. Sudana drove us through the narrow roads to avoid the traffic and I could see the pristine lifestyle of the Balinese people. One needs to spend at least a few days to appreciate and explore the heartland of Bali and Ubud. Sudana took a shortcut and we drove through some lonely roads, often taking sharp turns to match the curves. Wallah… suddenly I could see the rice terraces in front of us. Beautiful! I have seen rice terraces in Sapa, Vietnam during an earlier trip. I admit they were gorgeous. But there was a difference. The rice terraces in Sapa stood as a supreme beauty on their own. They would make you feel 'Wow'! Here in Bali, the rice terraces were nestled among homes, sometimes spread between coconut plantations. They were a part of the dwellings. The terraces were designed nicely in a staircase formation to manage the slope of the terrain. And oh boy, the surroundings were so green! In the fading daylight, the collage of the rolling rice terraces, the village homes, and the nearby streets with shops and eateries made them a picture-perfect 'serenity now' canvas of Ubud. I treasured that moment so near and dear to my heart. Till today when I close my eyes, I can clearly see those rice terraces in the fading daylight. I was absorbed in my thoughts when Desi reminded me that it was time to move on. Yes, I had made a deal with Desi and had told her that I would like to visit her home and family when I went to Ubud and she had agreed. To me, this is the best way to know local cultures and their way of life. This is the best gift for me whenever I travel abroad.

"Remember, we have to pick up Kadek and go for dinner after this," Desi reminded me on our way to her home.

"*Damn, why hadn't I planned to stay at least one more extra day in Ubud?*" I cursed myself. I wish I had known how beautiful the place was!

"Of course, we will pick up Kadek," I replied while looking outside.

The sky was fairly dark which meant that Mother Nature would empty herself soon. There had been a downpour before we reached Desi's home. We could see that the road was wet. I was lucky, I hadn't faced any rain in Bali till then, although it was November and it was the rainy season there. Otherwise, all my water sports would have been washed away! I was fortunate!

On the way, Desi explained about the most important Balinese festival, the Galungan ceremony. The festival goes on for ten days ending with Kuningan. Again, it's a celebration of the triumph of good against evil, right over wrong. The festival had ended just a couple of weeks earlier. Penjors, the bamboo poles decorated with coconut leaves, were still visible in front of the houses. I made a mental note that I would plan to be here a few weeks earlier to witness the ceremony in my future trips.

"This is my home," said Desi and pointed to a house close by while Sudana parked the car.

I was delighted. It was so wonderful to meet her whole family. She lived in a joint family, her parents, aunt, niece, and grandmother, all lived together. I was fortunate to meet her grandmother. She had passed away at the time of the writing of this book. Her mother was such a sweet lady! She talked to me gently with a smile on her face and then excused herself to arrange snacks and coffee for me. I was amazed by the touch of South Asian hospitality! Similar to other Balinese homes, the house sat in a big compound with many shrines spread across it. Each shrine was devoted to a certain God and Goddess. But one shrine, as Sudana had explained to me the day before, was dedicated to the departed souls in the family. In Bali, festivals and rituals occur almost year-round. There was a ritual coming soon and her father was busy preparing food for that. After the coffee, Desi showed me around the house. I loved it. I could spend many more hours chatting here with the family but it was already pretty dark outside and it was a bit of a drive to Sanur from Desi's home. We knew that Kadek would be waiting for us. I was saddened to say goodbye to everyone. All of them came to see us off. I was reluctant to leave. They had treated me, a foreigner from a distant land, with so much love and affection. I felt like I was home. They were indeed a happy Balinese family with a touch of love everywhere.

"Thank you, Desi," I whispered and got into the car.

The day ended with a lovely dinner in a classy restaurant in Sanur. Some locals performed the Balinese dance. We were among the last patrons to leave Legong Restaurant. This was it! It was time to say goodbye to Bali. I had an early morning flight to Labuan Bajo the next day. My heart sank a bit. I had fallen in love with Bali. I had thoroughly enjoyed my fun-filled days. But it was not the fun or the place by itself that I was going to miss, it was the people who had extended their arms to welcome me into their world. They had made a difference!

"So, this is it?" asked Kadek while we hugged and said goodbye.

"I suppose, my friend. All good times come to an end," I smiled.

"Not quite, not yet… we made a deal, remember!" smiled Desi.

"Of course!" I said, returning the smile.

Yes, we had already made a secret deal! More of that coming later.

When the Uber dropped me at the hotel, it was close to midnight!

Arriving in Bali

Wearing Sarong before entering temple

Main entrance to Besakih Temple

A view from the top

Barong dance

Wood carving and painting are popular in Bali

Sanur

*Desi Yanti, my
wonderful tour
organizer*

*Desi with her family
at home*

Paragliding in Bali

Having some fun with parasailing and waterboarding

Snorkeling and watersports are popular in Bali

Two:

Komodo island – Dragon's den

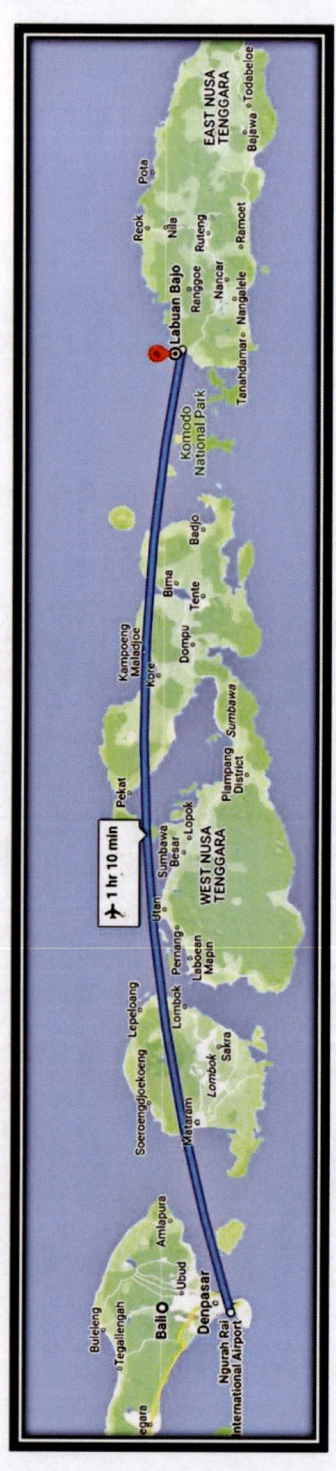

Say hello to the Komodo dragons – a species nearing extinction

o dragons really exist? Or are they a myth? A Google search told me that they were fictitious. But Komodo dragons do exist! Well, hardly, they are near extinction. These deadly beasts are the largest living lizards that roam around freely in a handful of islands in Indonesia. Komodo and Rinca islands in the Java Sea are two of those. I remember seeing this deadly lizard in the Bond movie, 'Skyfall'. But I wanted to see them in their natural habitat before they totally disappear from the face of the earth.

All I knew about Komodo island is that it is not too far from Bali. While planning for the trip, I didn't check the map nor did I have the faintest idea of how to travel there from Bali. I figured that an easy boat ride could be arranged and it might take a day or so to travel there. So I thought travelling back and forth from Bali would cost me two valuable days. I was sceptical as I was running on a tight schedule.

I decided to bring this up during my chat with Desi, "What shall I do? A boat from Bali would be too long a ride, isn't it? I can't spare the time!"

"Are you crazy? No one does that."

"Then?"

"Fly to Labuan Bajo from Bali, it's just over an hour's flight from Bali. Then you can take a boat from there to Komodo island. It's a four-hour boat ride from there. I will arrange the travel details for you."

"Bingo! Is it a regular service? How many in a boat?"

"You and your guide. Not too many tourists travel there, you know. You are the crazy one!" she chuckled over the phone.

"Hmm… is it safe?"

"Safe from what? Dragons are not safe for sure. Don't try to be a hero!" she began giggling.

"Will you come along with me?" I asked, hoping against hope.

"Hahaha, no way Sir. I have no interest in dating a dragon. You are on your own. I will arrange a good guide for you, don't worry."

But I did worry. A lonely journey over the Java Sea with some unknown people gave me an uneasy feeling! I didn't feel safe travelling there alone with all my cash. Before I left the restaurant in Sanur, I quietly handed Desi most of my dollars.

"Hey, what are you doing?" she asked, surprised.

"You are my banker. I am not travelling alone to the Java Sea with a pocketful of dollars."

"So, why are you giving these to me?"

"Return them when we meet again. You know where!"

"You are crazy! Nothing will happen!"

"Bad things do happen. Please don't say 'No.'"

She was a bit reluctant but accepted the cash. She counted the bills and wrote down the total on top of the envelope and asked, "Why me?"

"Because I trust you," I told her, meeting her eyes.

She gave me her usual lovely innocent smile and we said goodbye.

I'm used to taking early morning flights on my travels. I do that often. Even for my work, I sometimes have to run to the airport in the wee hours. So it was not an issue for me. My taxi was already waiting when I reached the front desk of the hotel to check out. The sun hadn't come up yet and it was dark, but the darkness was slowly fading away and the dawn was tiptoeing on the horizon. The taxi headed out to Denpasar Airport through Bali's lonely roads. I had checked in for my flight well in advance. I settled down with a cup of coffee and had a quick breakfast after the security check. When I was about to finish my coffee, I heard the departure announcement over the PA system. I checked my watch and thought that it couldn't be my flight. The announcement seemed a bit premature. Anyway, I shrugged, finished my coffee, and headed towards the boarding gate. Oh my God, wasn't I glad that I had reached the gate on time? The turbo aircraft of Garuda Airlines took off ten minutes before schedule! I was stunned! I was used to flight delays. I didn't know that a flight could depart ahead of schedule! Actually, this was not the first time this happened to me with Garuda Airlines. Later I had a similar experience in Jakarta airport when I was leaving for Borneo. Perhaps it's the trademark of Garuda Airlines, who knows? I was glad that I had reported well in advance. I made a mental note that I should check in early for all my Garuda flights from there on.

The flight took off and circled over Bali to set its flight path for Labuan Bajo. The sun was just coming over the horizon and struggling behind a curtain of clouds. Once the seatbelt sign was off, I leaned closer to the window to take a last look at Bali fading away behind the morning clouds. I sighed as gazed out. I get especially nostalgic when I have to leave a place that is close to my heart. It's a 'soul place' where I feel at home. I remembered that I had the same feeling when I left Hanoi in Vietnam a couple of years ago. I felt like I was leaving a city I loved, one that I will never see again. Truly, it's the people who make all the difference in this world. They are the ones who make a special place in your heart, not the place itself. Gazing through the window I could see the last traces of the landmarks in Bali with the causeways and lagoons squeezing in from the Indian Ocean, looking like a picture postcard. As the plane ascended high into the sky, my short-lived trip to Bali which was so close to my heart, faded away behind the early morning clouds. I sighed deeply and leaned against my seat.

It was a short flight to Labuan Bajo, just over an hour. The sky was clear when we landed. It is the western tip of the beautiful Flores island and the gateway to the Komodo and Rinca islands. Surprise, surprise! I didn't realize that a welcome dance by the locals was waiting for us in the arrival lounge. Wow! What a welcome show! The entire wall of the lounge was painted with beautiful Flores island images. The girls, wearing costumes to match the ambience, danced like beautiful little angels! I had never been to Hawaii, but I had seen their dance before. The dance in Labuan Bajo reminded me of the typical Hawaiian-style choreography. This lovely reception upon arrival definitely set the mood. I had never experienced anything like it at any airport in my life. I thought that it was a great concept to attract tourists! I enjoyed the performance thoroughly while waiting for the luggage.

Alas! I later realised that the performance was actually meant for some senior government officials travelling with us. Nevertheless, my mood was not dampened. The performance was indeed beautiful even though it was organized for a different reason. Anyway, the lovely reception set the tone for the day, I must say.

My tour guide Gonzales was waiting outside the terminal. He was a well-mannered quiet man in his mid-thirties. After our mutual greetings were done, we walked to the jeep waiting outside in the airport's parking lot.

"We have to pick up some odds and ends on the way," said Gonzalez as he started his car.

"Sure thing! What do we need?"

"Snorkelling gear and some drinks."

"*Snorkelling again!*" I thought. "Snorkelling where? I thought I am here to see the Komodo dragons," I said, surprised.

"Yeah, once we are done, we will do a bit of snorkelling on our way back. It will be hot and humid! You will enjoy it, you know," he smiled while keeping his eyes on the road.

"Who gave you this idea?" I was curious.

"I discussed it with Desi," he replied sheepishly.

"*Ah, the cat is out of the bag, Queen of Bali,*" I reflected silently and smiled.

Cool! Looks like Gonzalez already had a plan. But I needed to hear it, so I started the conversation while he drove.

"How long will it take us?"

"How long will what take us?" he glanced at me.

"To reach Komodo island."

"Oh, it depends on the sea. If it is not choppy, we will make it in four hours, give or take 10-15 minutes here and there."

"And we go straight to the island?"

"Where else?" he laughed. "You are in the middle of nowhere," he said as he seemed to relish my ignorance!

"True. Are you a regular on this route?" I asked as I wanted to feel a bit comfortable while travelling with this unknown fellow.

"That's all I have been doing for the last two years, my friend! Relax, you will be fine."

Probably Gonzalez felt my uneasiness. He parked the car near an outdoor rental place and rented some gear. I was sure Desi had arranged it. Gonzalez also picked up some drinks from a store selling beer. I watched him from near the counter.

He noticed and said, "There will be nothing around there. You wouldn't get any drinks for the next two days, even if you are dying to get one! It will be hot and muggy over there."

"*Sure, he is a regular in this route!*" I thought and relaxed. He knew what he was doing.

We got on a large boat. There were three decent bedrooms side by side on the main floor with the stairwell going to the upper deck from the starboard side. The kitchen and extra rooms were below the main level. Some chairs were placed casually on a closed patio on the main floor.

"How many crew members do you have, Gonzalez?" I asked him while checking the place out.

"I have three people on my crew including the chef! Well, they are not exactly my crew. I work for Adventure Indonesia. But I am the boss here," he grinned.

"*Yes, of course,* I thought while getting to know his role! "So, this our home for the next two days," I said, turning around.

"Yup," he replied while looking out of the window.

"And we will have our lunch and dinner also in here, I suppose," I said and immediately realized that it was a stupid question.

"Unless you have other ideas," he eyed me with a smirk. I didn't comment and just returned the smile.

"We will arrive at noon. We will first finish our lunch in the boat, and then head out," he continued.

"You are the boss, I will go with the flow," I said. It was my turn to grin.

That made him happy and he laughed. Good, he had a sense of humour! Otherwise, it would be a boring sea journey for the next two days.

The crew took the anchor out. Soon we boarded the boat and headed out on a sunny morning sailing over the aqua-blue water of the Java Sea. Rolling hills jutted out from the sea here and there. I could see the clear sandy beaches where the rolling hills met the sea. The hills were pretty barren, unlike Bali where greenery was everywhere. I asked Gonzalez if people lived on those islands.

"Not really... except in a few places. Some of those are fishing villages," he replied. After a pause, he added, "There are a few caves and falls close to Labuan Bajo, you know."

He seemed to expect my response but I just nodded.

"Some come here for holidays. There are wooden cottages and facilities, you know," he continued.

Then he asked after a pause, "Are you interested?"

I guess he expected me to spend a couple of days there on my way back. The poor guy had no idea how tight my schedule was and I had no intentions of cancelling my flight to Yogyakarta in order to spend some extra time in Labuan Bajo.

"I hear you. But not now Gonzalez, maybe another time," I told him while gazing at the horizon across the blue Java Sea.

The sea was not choppy, so the ride was actually very smooth and comfortable. The only reason I came travelling this far was to quench my childhood desire to see the Komodo dragons in real life. But the beautiful landscape outside the window was a bonus. I loved the blue sky reflected on the tranquil Java Sea and the lonely rolling hills that jutted out everywhere.

It was a serene and peaceful canvas 'far from the madding crowd' and away from the cacophony of the tourist bazaar. I checked my phone. I was still getting a Wi-Fi signal, which meant that the internet was working. So this was a good time to check and respond to some messages till the signal dropped. This gave me some time to catch up with the rest of the world while the cook prepared the tasty meal.

Gonzalez called me when the lunch was ready. Wow, I was pleasantly surprised by the freshly cooked and delicious meal! I am used to simple food most of the time when travelling. Sometimes I survive on some dry fruits, cookies, and a bottle of water and I am happy with it. I carry them in my backpack. I was definitely not expecting such an exquisite feast of seafood cooked with fresh vegetables and rice on the side. I thanked Gonzalez and his team. Of course, hats off to Desi too for organizing this so thoughtfully!

We arrived near Komodo island right after noon.

"We have to pick up a guide from the Ranger's office," Gonzalez said.

"Do we need one?" I asked.

"Oh, yes. It's the rule. You cannot get inside the park without one. Also, you have to select the track that you want to hike on. There are short, medium, and long tracks," he paused for a moment and looked at me. He hadn't quite finished yet. "Another thing. It's quite dangerous out there. The guides know best."

I got his point. We picked a guide from the Ranger's office. Soon I found that Gonzalez was right. The trails often ran through dense bushes and trees. Often it was impossible to see what was lurking behind those bushes. The beasts could easily camouflage themselves inside the bush and it was easy to fall prey to them. They are carnivores and they would not leave anything untouched except the head. The dragons roaming all over the island pretty much fed on pigs, deer, water buffaloes i.e. any living creature. Attacks on humans were rare, but they had happened before. The dragons do go out hunting in the daytime so it was quite possible we would encounter one. I was sure they wouldn't be in the mood to say 'Hello' to me when they were hungry.

The guide was walking in front of us. He stopped suddenly and his long stick blocked my step.

"Shhh! Stop right there," he whispered without looking at us.

We stopped and stood still. Wallah! There it was! A beast weighing over 200 pounds was just staring at us from behind a distant bush. Wow! I was mesmerized! This was the beast that had roamed this planet millions of years ago and now I was looking at it. Alive! I noticed its flat head and powerful front legs. Its forked tongue came out every few seconds with lightning speed. I knew that Komodo dragons sample the air with their forked tongues and then touch their tongues to the roof of their mouths. That is how they sense where their prey is.

I figured the beast was close to 10 ft long. Its tail was very thick, like a crocodile's. It was swaying its head right and left looking for food and then it started moving towards us, thumping its heavy feet. I was standing with the guide at a ten o'clock position and Gonzales was in the opposite direction. I felt a pull on my arm.

The guide warned me, "Move back, don't go so close."

Gonzalez had told me earlier that the dragons can run at a speed of 20 kph for a short distance and can outrun their prey when in a vantage position. Then they spring up on their heavy feet to knock down the prey and pretty much shred them to pieces with their shark-like sharp teeth. Even if a prey somehow gets away from its clutches, it does not survive long. The saliva of the Komodo dragon contains around 50 strains of toxic substances with deadly bacteria. The prey dies of blood poisoning in a short time. The dragon also sprays venom on the legs of water buffaloes to paralyze and then kill them.

I learned certain rules from Gonzalez during the boat ride.

Rule No. 1: Don't go in front of a dragon or get too close. They can run swiftly and catch you quickly or spew saliva. Walk a large semi-circle and go behind the beast.

Rule No. 2: If you have an open wound or if you are a woman who is menstruating, stay as far as you can. They have an incredibly strong sense of smell and once they smell blood, they will hunt down and kill the prey.

I came close to its tail and kept my camera ready. Click, Click! Again I felt a pull and the guide dragged me back.

"You are too close," he said.

I had squatted too close to the beast. It suddenly turned around with lightning speed and made a move towards me. I sprang back from my squatting position and ran back to keep some distance. If I had toppled at that moment, the story would have been different. I was fortunate that I made it. The beast was looking at me intensely, its tongue flicking in and out.

Gonzalez came to me and gave me a stern look, "Don't try to be a hero, Mister."

I knew what I had done was foolish.

I looked at him and said, "Thanks, I'll be careful."

Gonzalez nodded. No, I was not going to argue with the guide. I did not want to be a hero and offer myself as the lunch menu for the beast. I stepped back as the guide had ordered me. The dragon finally came to an open area and then walked into the bush looking for food. I sighed with relief. The excitement and the rush of adrenaline were exhausting.

We started our hike again, often through the bush and up the hill. Sometimes the bush was not very dense and we could see the Java Sea at a distance. We met a few of the beasts during the hike. I was thankful that we had a guide. He warned us as soon as his trained eyes spotted one. Had we been alone, I am sure we would have stepped right into the 'dragon's den.' Most probably I wouldn't be sharing this story with you.

We continued our mostly uphill trek. It was tiring and we were all sweating. I stopped to catch my breath and looked up. The tropical sun was blazing over our heads and the humidity was not making it easy. I was thirsty and looked for my water bottle in my backpack. I couldn't find it.

"Where the hell was it? Did it fall out anywhere?" I thought.

Then I remembered! I didn't want to carry any luggage other than my camera just in case I had to run for my life. I didn't realize that this could be so strenuous. Lesson learned! Never leave the essentials behind before a trek. Nevertheless, I must say that it was a good day for hunting Komodo dragons and Mother Nature had been kind so far.

Rinca island was a two-hour boat ride from there. Although we selected a short hike, it took us the better part of the day to cover the trek. It was almost four o'clock and there was no time to make it to the island on the same day. We anchored our boat near some small islands in the Java Sea away from Komodo island and called it a day. I went to the upper deck and settled down to chill with a drink. A crimson-red sun was going down the horizon over the Java Sea. It was absolutely quiet. There was no sound other than the small waves splashing on our boat. A gorgeous sunset illuminated the horizon and I enjoyed the serenity while sipping my cold beer. Thanks to Gonzalez! He sure knew what would be needed at the end of a hot and humid day. Soon darkness fell all around us. I had had a long day since I had left Bali early in the morning and it was time for me to wind down after dinner. I checked my watch. It was only 9 pm. Indeed, it was too early for bed. So I climbed to the upper deck and grabbed a chair to quietly enjoy the darkness. There was just another small boat anchored at a distance. I could see the dim light coming from the boat but didn't pay much attention. There was no other sign of civilization!

Ah, what a calm evening! It was time to enjoy the darkness and dive into star gazing. Gonzalez had retired to his room after a long day and I heard the occasional sound of utensils from downstairs. Perhaps the crew members were still working in the kitchen below. Our boat was anchored about half a mile from another island. It was totally quiet. There were no sounds other than the occasional ones of birds trying to settle down for the night on the nearby island. The air was still. These are the times of solitude when tranquillity slowly creeps into the mind and one wants to be left alone to ponder.

I remembered Denys Finch from the movie 'Out of Africa' telling Karen Blixen sitting under a vast African sky in total darkness, "I don't want to live someone else's idea of how to live."

Denys was right! I had been fortunate enough to experience some of these special moments in my life. I will never forget those evenings over Ha Long Bay in Vietnam, or in Tharn Thong Lodge in Northern Thailand where sitting under a starry sky, the darkness from the rolling hills used to slowly spread into my mind. I will never forget the night when I spent hours on a moonlit night outside my tent in Masaimara in Africa and enjoyed the silver drops from heaven on my head. Those were unforgettable moments. I live for such moments!

Suddenly I woke up from my deep trance and heard a faint sound. It was a splashing sound coming from a short distance near the starboard. It was dark and I couldn't see anything. But the sound was steady and getting closer. I stood up and tried to trace its origin carefully. Suddenly I realized that it was the sound of hand strokes made when someone swims in water.

"Nha, who would be so crazy to swim in a dark sea in the middle of the night," I brushed the thought aside.

"Is anyone up there?" shouted a guy in English from the water below.

Oh, my God, there was indeed a person swimming in the dark. For heaven's sake, why on earth would a sensible person swim in the dark sea? And swimming from where? There was nothing close by other than the boat at a distance. Did someone live on those islands? Pirates? Robbery? If someone wanted to rob and kill us in the middle of the Java Sea, no one in the world would ever know what happened.

I shouted back, "Who is there?"

"We are from the other boat," came the reply.

Oh no! That meant two guys at least. I climbed down the ladder from the upper deck and called for Gonzalez. He came out of his room, half asleep. One of the crew members came running with a lantern and torch. We could see that one guy was hanging from the starboard holding some kind of mechanical support.

"Who are you and what the hell are you doing there in the middle of the night?" I asked him while training my torchlight on his face.

"We are from the other boat. Just chilling out a bit. We came to say 'Hi.'"

Now the other guy also swam next to the first man and was hanging from the starboard, still half submerged in water. Probably they were tourists and crazy ones. But this was not funny! Some guys had come across in the middle of the night to say 'Hi!' Whoever they were, I thought the guys were insane and the whole idea of swimming in a dark sea was ridiculous! Who knows what kind of dangerous marine species lurked around in the deep sea? Taking a chance by swimming in the dark in an unknown world was nothing but asking for trouble.

I shouted, "This is not funny, you know! I think you guys should go back to your boat. It doesn't sound like a good idea to swim in the dark sea."

I moved away from the starboard side of the deck, just to discourage the unwanted visitors. Gonzalez was a cool cat and was watching the guys without saying a word.

Once the guys swam back, he opened his mouth, "Don't worry, they wouldn't do us any harm. Not that type."

"How do you know?" I asked, perplexed.

"I cover this route regularly," he said and walked back to his cabin.

I was not so sure, but I trusted Gonzalez and his instinct. No doubt I was a bit shaken. I felt a bit uneasy, wondering about those crazy guys. The other boat was anchored quite far from us, at least half a mile. Swimming such a long distance in a dark sea all the way just to say 'Hi' was insane, no matter how calm the sea was. Anyway, I tried to put my discomfort aside as I wanted to enjoy the solitude and darkness. But my mood was already spoiled and anxiety overshadowed my mind. So I called it a night and went to my cabin. I locked the door before I went to bed. No, I was not taking any chances. I knew the flimsy cabin door and its fragile lock were not secure protection if someone wanted to break in but it still offered some level of comfort. With that thought I slowly drifted to sleep.

I woke up at my usual time, around 4:30 am. No, I hadn't set any alarm, it was just my habit. I had a mental alarm perhaps. One of the crew members was already up that early, but Gonzalez was fast asleep. I slowly climbed up the stairs to the upper deck. Thousands of stars were spread like diamonds in the sky... the bright Orion constellation, Sirius, Vega... they were all there! My anxiety from last night's visitors had vanished by then and my mind was fresh. The cool breeze from the sea was brushing my cheeks. The star-filled night hovered over the tranquil Java Sea early in the morning. I wanted to spend this time of the day on my own. Just me... alone and deeply absorbed within me. This morning was mine. I wanted to witness the dawn over the Java Sea alone. Slowly the darkness faded away and the stars said goodbye.

The day broke with a fresh promise as though saying, "I am here." Slowly the sky transformed into a collage of hundreds of beautiful colours. Mother Nature had painted the canvas of the sky with glorious colours. A few more minutes and the orange-crimson sun jumped up like a ball from the sea on the distant horizon. I was grateful that I had lived to see that moment.

"Good morning!" I didn't quite notice when Gonzalez came and stood behind me.

I turned around and returned his greetings.

"Did you have a good night's sleep?" he asked me.

"Same as usual, how about you?"

"Couldn't be better. I know you were troubled last night by the sudden visitors. Don't worry about them. Hope you are not stressed."

I was surprised that I was not bothered by that incident anymore. Perhaps the daylight had freshened my mind. Now I was more curious about them.

"What about those guys? Are these people crazy swimming around in a dark sea?" I asked him.

"I have seen many crazy types in the last eight years in this sea, my friend."

"Have you ever had any incidents?"

"Close, but not quite. Breakfast?"

Gonzalez asked the crew members to serve breakfast on the open deck. Toast, scrambled eggs and fried asparagus with orange juice were the perfect start to the day and they lifted my spirits for the next stop, Rinca island.

Rinca island and the final hunt

From where we had anchored our boat, it was a two-hour boat ride to Rinca island. We started fairly early, so the weather wasn't that hot yet. The breeze from the calm sea was cool enough to make it a comfortable ride. When we went near the island, it appeared to be more barren than Komodo island. We anchored our boat near it and walked on the board walk. We were the only tourists.

At Komodo island, the arrangements for tourists had been better with guides and office rooms located right at the entrance of the main gate and more tourist activities were notable as we were closing to the main entrance to Komodo island. At Rinca, it was a long walk over desolate and barren land to reach the main gate and only after crossing it, we saw the small office of the warden. Without the right guidance, it was easy to get lost there. I was happy that Gonzalez was with me and we started walking towards the main gate. It was just mid-morning and the sun was already hot. While walking on the barren pathway, I compared it to Komodo island and felt that the latter was greener and leafier. I could see the green hills of Rinca island standing silently at a distance on that sticky hot day. Once we arrived at the main entrance, we saw the display of skulls from dead animals hanging from the trunk of a tree, a grim reminder of the danger ahead. They were the remnants from the dragon feasts.

The office of the warden was just a small tin shed and a handful of people were relaxing around a table. Not many tourists from Bali travelled to these desolate islands just to see the dragons. Some diehard ones might but a majority of them visited only Komodo island and returned to Labuan Bajo. Very few of them take the trouble of travelling for another two hours by boat to come to Rinca. But that suited me just fine.

"We need a guide to take us to the trail," Gonzalez told the people at the warden's office.

"Short, medium or long trail?" asked one of them, casually leaning on a chair.

He seemed to be the warden here, in charge of the guides. I was aware that I had to catch a flight in the afternoon from Labuan Bajo, so we couldn't afford to go on a long trail. After discussing the logistics with Gonzalez for a few seconds, we settled for a short hike. The warden nodded to one of the guides who stood up from a chair and came with us. We paid the fees and headed out to the trail. Once we went up the trail, the barren hills that we had seen from a distance slowly came into view and I found that they were not so barren after all. The bush and shrubs became denser and I could see leafy trees. We first halted not due to the dragon but because of the aggressive stance of a water buffalo. The buffalo was grazing by the side of the trail and the angry-looking mammal suddenly dashed towards us as soon as it saw us.

"Relax and wait," the guide whispered.

It was the instinct of the poor animal. It has learned the truth of life here i.e. survival of the fittest. We waited and let the buffalo relax. Once it realized that we are not a threat, it slowly walked away.

We saw the first dragon dens near the trail, but there were no signs of them. They were probably out hunting. Then my guide slowed down and I almost missed it. The beast was resting in a bush, just 6 feet away from us. It was totally camouflaged by shrubs and bushes. The same thing had happened earlier on Komodo island. The beasts hide themselves so well that it is hard to spot them unless one is trained to do so. I was thankful that we had a trained guide. Had my guide not been with me, my skull would have been on display at the main entrance for the viewing of future tourists. We slowly circled the dragon's den and took a detour from the main trail to avoid the deadly beast and climbed up further.

We hiked for almost an hour but were not lucky enough to spot anything. Indeed, we tracked a few babies on our way back to the main gate, but that was it. I must say that we were luckier in Komodo island where we had encountered a number of them. Maybe it had a much larger dragon population than Rinca and that could be the reason why tourists flocked more often to Komodo island. But since we just took a short hike here, my judgment may not be totally correct. Perhaps, we might have spotted more beasts if we had opted for the medium or long hike. Anyway, we knew our limits since we were short of time. I had no regrets.

Gonzalez pointed out that it was time for us to leave. We thanked the warden when we reached his office and started walking on the lonely pathway outside the main gate towards our boat. I glanced at the display of the animal skulls once more as we stepped out from the cordoned area of the dragon habitat. I did feel a bit safer, but I was sure that I would miss them.

"Miss them? Are you nuts?" Gonzalez laughed when I shared my thoughts with him.

Not really, but it gave me a thrill to watch those deadly beasts who have roamed around this planet for millions of years! I was fortunate enough to observe them since they probably would be a footnote in history fifty years from now. I certainly hoped I was wrong! I have observed them closely for the last two days. They are dangerous creatures and wouldn't show their prey any mercy. However, unlike some other predators, they are predictable to a certain extent. Once you played by their rules, you will live to tell their stories to others as I am sharing them with you.

It was close to noon and my flight was due to leave at 4 pm. It would take about an hour and a half to travel to Labuan Bajo from there. That gave me just a bit of time to do some snorkelling in the crystal-clear water of the Java Sea. We anchored the boat near another island and I could see the beautiful sandy beach of the island right from the deck. It was so tempting! It reminded me of some of the beaches in Nusa Dua that I loved. But compared to Bali, there were no other tourists. We could see another boat anchored far away, but no tourist activities.

"Isn't that great? The whole beach is for us," said Gonzalez, grinning at me.

"Just to let you know Gonzalez, I don't know how to swim," I told him flatly.

"Don't worry, we are just going to snorkel a bit," he assured me.

"Well, I do worry. Sometimes I cannot even float properly."

I cautiously added the word 'sometimes,' because my latest success in Bali had improved my confidence in snorkelling to some extent.

"Hey, I'm here and I will be right behind you," he said while strapping the vest around his chest.

I wore my snorkelling gear and followed Gonzalez as he climbed down the boat to the water using a ladder hooked to the boat. The water was not deep where the boat was anchored and we could move easily towards the beach. The water was shallow and I could walk in the waist-level water as one does in a swimming pool. There was certainly no fear of drowning here. Slowly I pushed my head down into the water and enjoyed my snorkelling session. There were no tourists and I felt free to try it out at my own pace. In a way, I was glad that not too many tourists came here to see the dragons. This gave me a chance to practice 'swimming 101' which my travel blog friend M.J. insisted that I should do before coming to Bali. The water was so clear that I could even count the pebbles lying on the sea bed.

Gonzalez was swimming close to me at the beginning, just to make sure that I was okay. When he saw that I was trying to find my rhythm, he left me alone. Then he swam further away but I was not afraid anymore. He must have realized that there was no way I could drown in the water which was only chest deep. We snorkelled for almost an hour before we headed to the boat. It was a welcome respite from the heat and the sticky weather. I felt really refreshed before heading out to the airport. Needless to say, the chef had prepared a steaming lunch when we boarded the boat after the swim. What a treat! There was rice to go with stir-fried mixed vegetables and fried prawns with a tossed salad on the side! I must admit, I was hungry after the workout in the water and enjoyed the delicious food thoroughly.

Once we reached Labuan Bajo, I climbed out of the boat with my backpack and the luggage and said goodbye to Gonzalez and his crew. I liked Gonzalez. He was a cool cat and he had planned everything, including an hour's relaxation by including snorkelling in my tight schedule. My type of guy! He truly has a nomadic lifestyle! I'm not sure if I could handle spending days out in Java Sea with nothing around me except the lonely islands. But I admired him. It is not easy to live this lonely lifestyle away from family. It's not for everyone. He dropped me at the airport and wished me a great flight. We shook hands as I headed to the gate. I turned around for the last time at the gate and saw him waving at me from a distance, still smiling. I am not sure if our paths would cross again, but I will always remember the moments he spent with me. While I hop from one place to another on this seemingly infinite planet, these moments of friendship are my real treasures.

"Take only memories, leave only footsteps," I reminisced.

The flight took off on that warm, sunny afternoon leaving Flores Island behind. The sky was clear and the aircraft made a circle to set its direction. From my window seat, I could see the small islands dotted all over the Java Sea. Among those, somewhere down below, would be Komodo and Rinca islands, baking in the afternoon sun. I closed my eyes and imagined that the huge lizards were roaming around looking for food behind the bushes, flicking their tongues and swaying their heads. After their meal, they would slowly return to their den after the sun went down.

I may return to Bali someday. Would I visit the lizards again? Maybe, maybe not! I wanted to see them at least once, freely roaming around in their natural habitat before they became extinct. I was glad that I had made it. I had fulfilled my dream. I loved the tranquil Java Sea, its calm crystal-clear water and the landscape dotted with so many desolate islands where one could spend days watching the days fade in and out, totally alone. Right at that moment, I envied Gonzalez!

Flores Island

Reception at Labuan Bajo Airport

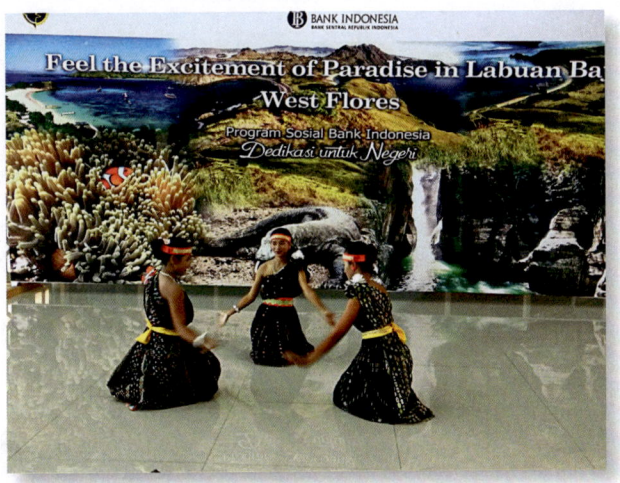

Gonzalez, my tour guide for Komodo Island

Komodo National Park

Komodo dragon

Walking trails in Komodo and Rinca islands

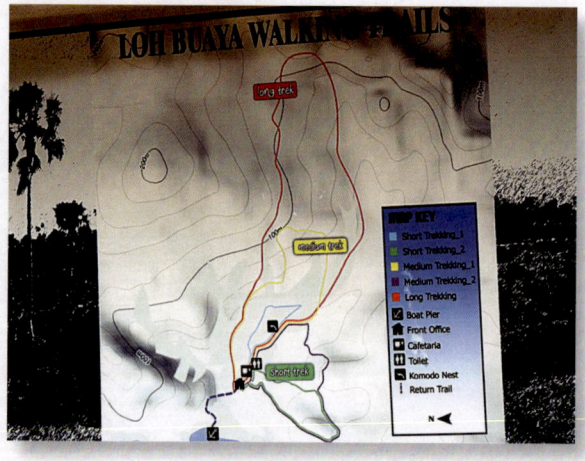

Entrance to Rinca island

Sunrise over Java Sea

Three:

Yogyakarta – Walking through history

The magnificent Borobudur and Prambanan temples

The flight from Labuan Bajo touched down at Bali and my connecting Garuda flight to Yogyakarta was at 6 pm from there. It was a short flight of just over an hour and we landed at the Yogyakarta Adisucipto International Airport at 7:30 pm. Though it was less than 1500 km from Labuan Bajo, it was a different world. Rich in cultural heritage and with footprints of history everywhere, it was a sharp contrast to the isolation of the Komodo and Rinca islands.

No, I'm not a history buff and adventure is in my blood. But don't get me wrong. It's not that history doesn't interest me at all! I am not talking about my history class in school days. Those were boring. Now that I do travel to various places in the world, it's different. I need to correlate the history of the place to what I see and experience. I often read about ancient cultures in my leisure time. Those are interesting and I enjoy them more than the history classes in my school. My aspiration to explore the fusion of cultures in Southeast Asia drags me often to this part of the world. I became interested in Buddhism during my first trip to Thailand years ago. I tried to dig into some unusual destinations in Thailand away from mainstream tourist attractions. My interest in Buddhism and how it had blended with the Hindu religion in some Asian countries grew deeper when I learned more about Angkor Wat in Cambodia. At the same time, I wanted to explore the migration of Indian culture to Indonesia and learn about its synthesis with Buddhism. From my studies of Angkor Wat and Borobudur Temple, I learned that the archaeology of the Borobudur and Prambanan Temples in Yogyakarta was a fusion of the Buddhist and Hindu faith that occurred at the time of the Khmer Empire in Cambodia. Javanese culture might also have had some influence. That was one of the reasons I was curious to learn more about Borobudur which is now a UN Heritage site. It had been on my to-do list for quite some time and I was excited that I had finally made it!

"A day trip to Yogyakarta is not going to work out well for you, my friend. There are many things to see," Desi had warned me when I was planning the trip.

Actually, I knew that too. There were cultural shows like the Ramayana ballet available at a very reasonable price in Yogyakarta. If I had planned an extra evening there, I would have loved to watch it.

"I wish I could, Desi. Unfortunately, that's all the time I could afford in Yogyakarta," I told her.

I asked her to book me a flight to Yogyakarta from Labuan Bajo. I flew in just for a short day trip to Yogyakarta, more commonly known as Jogjakarta or simply Jogja. The flight landed during a heavy downpour, the wheels splashing water from the runway. I looked through my window as the aircraft slowly taxied to the terminal building. I was not that surprised to see that there was no air bridge, as many smaller airports around the world don't have one.

"Well, I guess I have to make a short run to the terminal," I told myself.

I knew I would get wet in this heavy rain. When it rains in this part of the world, it's not a drizzle, it pours. Surprise, surprise! At the bottom of the stairwell, a guy waited with a bunch of umbrellas and was handing one to each passenger. When we reached the terminal building, another guy collected them from us. What a novel idea to serve the people! Necessity is the mother of invention! It's not a stylish approach but it's a practical one and it works! To me, that's all that matters! Needless to say, I was thankful I was not wet.

I picked up my luggage from the carousel and stepped out of the luggage area. My English-speaking guide was waiting at the arrival lounge with my name tag. The flight was reasonably full. Jogja is not as busy a tourist destination as Bali, but it gets a fair amount of traffic and many of the passengers on the flight were locals. So, there weren't many pick-up services waiting at the arrival lounge.

"Come with me, Sir," said the gentleman and asked me to follow him.

I was happy to see my airport pickup.

"Good, things were falling into place," I thought.

I felt comfortable that I had transportation ready to go to the hotel. The car was just waiting outside the arrival terminal parking lot. Once we reached the car, he introduced me to the driver and waved 'Goodbye' to me! I was a bit surprised.

Why had he waited all this time in the arrival lounge just to take me to the car and then bid me goodbye? Why couldn't the driver pick me up instead?

I was puzzled and thought, *"Maybe the car was in a tow-away zone and the driver needed to be there to look after the car."*

Ok, that explains it perhaps. But hang on! Then why did the other guy leave right away? We could have dropped him off on our way to the hotel. Something was not right. Maybe this was the custom here, I don't know.

I got into the car with all these thoughts whirling in my mind. Anyway, whatever it was, I didn't care anymore! I shrugged, greeted the driver and threw my luggage beside me on the back seat and settled in.

"Hello!" I said.

The driver didn't respond, he just smiled! I asked him in English if he knew where to go. He gestured with his hand that he didn't. That could have two meanings. First, he literally didn't know where to go. That was not a problem, I could explain things to him and finding a hotel in a city was not an issue. My second interpretation was that he didn't know how to speak English. Now that could be troublesome.

"Hmmm! Well, perhaps it's time for me to try some Bahasa to figure it out!" I thought. After all, I learned a bit from Desi and Ninik.

"Apa kabar... How are you?" I started with an easy one!

That was a mistake! The elderly man grinned at me and responded with something that sounded like 'Selamat malam' which would mean 'Good Evening.' That would have been fine, but then the man started talking to me rapidly and I could hardly understand his accent. I was not sure whether he was speaking to me in Bahasa or some other Javanese language. He didn't seem to care whether I understood what he was saying. He probably thought that I was fluent in his language.

"*Damn! What a mistake! Why the hell did I start speaking to him in Bahasa?*" I cursed myself.

I had made a similar mistake while travelling in Costa Rica in the past. There I had tried my broken Spanish at the hotel front desk and then had to almost beg the receptionist to speak to me in English once he started speaking to me in fluent Spanish. Of course, it was obvious that I hadn't learned my lesson.

"*Smartass,*" I scolded myself. "Only English please," I said loudly.

We were at a stop light. He quietly turned around and stared blankly at me. I realized that I had hit a brick wall. I didn't have much choice other than trying to speak in my broken Bahasa to a guy who hardly knew any English.

"Bisa bicara bahasa Inggris?" I asked him whether he knew English.

He grinned. This meant that he didn't. Perfect! That meant the next day would be quite a day for us together! This guy was most likely my driver and guide! My limited knowledge of Bahasa wouldn't take me far. Indeed, I had a challenge on my hand. Fortunately, I didn't have to explain my destination. He showed me a paper where the hotel's address was marked. That means he had already been briefed. That was a relief! There was no more conversation as we drove. I had reached the limits of my knowledge of Bahasa and the guy had flatly rejected the idea of speaking in English, so there was no point in trying to have a conversation. I looked out of the window and noticed that the roads were narrow and shacks and small shops cramped both sides of the road. Most were closed at this hour. It took us about half an hour to reach the hotel which was not too bad. Once I got out of the car, I told him in English to come the next day at 8 am. I am not sure whether he understood me but he smiled and left. I tried to think about how I would make it work between us the next day.

"*Instead of sleeping tonight, I should perhaps learn how to use sign language,*" I thought.

After checking in, I immediately went to the dining hall as I was a bit hungry. My last meal had been at noon while riding the boat over the Java Sea. I looked around, but there was hardly anyone in the dining room.

"Sorry Sir, we are closed," said the waitress. She saw me waiting at the door.

"But it's not that late yet! It is just past 9:30 pm," I almost begged.

The girl gave me a sad look and apologized again. I realized that it was not my day! There was no point in arguing, I could see that she was not going to budge. I turned around and went out to look for something to eat. The rain had stopped by then. It was close to 10 pm and the road in front of the hotel was quite desolate. It was unlikely that any restaurant or roadside eatery would be open at this hour, but it was worth a try. Besides, I was there only for a night and the next day was going to be busy.

I planned to visit the Borobudur Temple in the morning and then rush to the Prambanan Temple in the early afternoon before heading back to the airport to catch my flight to Semarang. So this was my only chance to catch a quick glimpse of this place even at this hour. I walked for a mile or so while thinking about these things.

Sidewalks were generally off-limits. They were either occupied with shacks or people sleeping on them. So I had to often walk on the main road. It reminded me of some places in Kolkata where I had grown up. Often the sidewalks in Kolkata were occupied by vendors and were off-limits to pedestrians.

Yogyakarta is an old city and my hotel might have been located in a congested area. It is my experience that every city in this world has something unique to offer and I was sure Jogja wouldn't be an exception. I checked my watch, it was past 11 pm. The roads were empty and I was quite far from the hotel in an unknown city. There wasn't a soul within hundred yards whom I could call for help if I was in trouble. I couldn't find any fast food joint either. It was certainly not my day. I turned around, exhausted. Once back at the hotel, I opened a packet of cookies from the backpack, my lifesaver on rainy days. The bedside clock showed that it was close to midnight. I quickly checked my messages. It had been a long day and I knew that the next day would be another exhausting day and I needed to rest. Dealing with my driver would be another headache. Lying on the bed I kept thinking about how I should tackle my driver so that we could communicate without much grief. I had no idea when I fell asleep.

The next morning my driver showed up on time. I remained calm and showed him the itinerary which had Borobudur on it. I wasn't sure whether he could read English. So, I uttered the word Borobudur and he nodded. That means the guy who picked me up from the airport last night must have explained the itinerary to him. What a mess! I gestured for him to move. The driver nodded again and we headed out. The sky was gloomy and the roads were wet. It had rained again last night. That meant that it would be a humid day. Well, that was nothing new in this part of the world and I was getting used to it. The car was air-conditioned. That was a relief! It snaked through the cacophony of the rush hour traffic. It took us about forty minutes to get out of the city. The Borobudur Temple was outside the city limits and the roads started becoming wider and the traffic became less as soon as we left the city. The communication challenge with my driver continued. He didn't understand even a little bit of what I was trying to say in half English and half Bahasa. I couldn't understand his accent either.

"*Perfect combination*," I thought! After a while, I gave up and kept the conversation to a minimum to save both of us from unnecessary grief. "*I would be happy if he dropped me at the airport on time at the end of the trip*," I thought.

After parking the car in the temple parking lot, my driver guided me to the main entrance of a building which looked like a shopping plaza. By that time, we were using body language to understand each other! There was no point asking him where he was heading. I just followed him. I just hoped that he knew what he was doing. Aha! We had reached the ticket counter! Well, at least he knew the routine and where to start. I walked up to the counter.

"One ticket, please," I was relieved that the lady spoke English.

As I took my wallet out, the lady said, "This is the counter for local people only, Sir."

I was confused and looked at the driver. The lady then explained the situation to the driver. Oh, well, the driver was perhaps used to bringing only local tourists here, so it was not his fault. We walked to another building where there was another set of counters with a clear display 'For Foreign Tourists only.' I got my first jolt when I reached the counter for the entrance ticket. The ticket price for a foreigner was almost ten times the cost of the ticket for the locals. I flipped and protested to the girl at the counter.

"This is outrageous! It is almost ten times the ticket cost paid by the locals!" I was furious.

The girl saw my face and apologetically said, "Well Sir, I don't make the rules."

She was polite and well-trained in customer service. I am sure I was not the first one to complain about the ticket price. But I realized that she was actually right. She was just an employee there, doing her job. To be honest, this was not the only place where I had seen such a price differential for a foreigner. Once I visited the Taj Mahal in India and I paid way more than an Indian citizen would pay. It was the same story in Thailand when I visited the Grand Palace. It was free for Thai citizens. But why shall I blame only the Asian countries? Canada and US also charge foreign students hefty fees. This is their way of making money! I had never liked differential fees or charges, irrespective of the country. I called it 'differential treatment' of a non-citizen! In my view, there are other ways to make money, not necessarily by robbing tourists or taking undue advantage of poor students. Such people are actually helping the economy of the place when they visit it. Anyway, there was no point in arguing with the girl. Of course, I was not happy. I could have walked away, but that would have been a stupid thing to do after having travelled halfway around the world to see the temple. So I paid the listed price and purchased the ticket.

"Terima Kasih," I thanked the girl and walked towards the temple compound.

The driver gestured with his hand showing me the general direction in which he had parked the car. I nodded and sighed deeply with relief, glad that I was on my own. It was a lovely walk amid the leafy trees and lush green manicured lawn inside the compound. One thing I loved about travelling in tropical countries was the lush greenery everywhere wherever I went. Especially, the grass is so green in these places that it looks unreal as if someone has painted it. I passed by a large field; hundreds of Muslim girls, all wearing red clothing and scarves covering their heads were enjoying a workout on the sunny morning. The instructor and the girls were all dancing to the rhythm of music from a large boom box. It was a typical Zumba-style workout. As far as I could see, it was a sea of red waves swaying to the sound of music. Awesome! I was impressed to see the awareness about health among Muslim women there. I stood and watched them for a few minutes. This is what I like about travelling alone. No one drives me crazy. I spend the time the way I like it. It would have been fun to watch the beautiful show for some more time, but I knew that there was plenty for me to explore in the two temples in just half a day. So I walked up to the main entrance.

The Borobudur Temple Compound is a massive architectural marvel that was built in the 9ᵗʰ century A.D. The only other massive temple that one possibly could compare with this one is Angkor Wat in Cambodia. Angkor Wat is spread over a large area with many temples, whereas Borobudur is one large temple complex. It has nine levels which one can climb up to reach the top. I was glad that I didn't take a guide. It was more fun to enjoy this marvellous architecture on my own.

It started with a magnificent stone carving on the first level of the temple and as I climbed up, the display of the sculptures engraved in stone was fascinating. On each floor of the temple, there were several halls decorated with stone carvings. Each carving told the story of the bygone days. There were statues of Lord Buddha in every corner of the halls on each floor and also inside the domes or stupas. The stone carving on the temple was literally a depiction of the legendary Javanese culture that was the fusion of Buddhism and Indian civilization from the ancient Gupta dynasty. While strolling from hall to hall, I could see the restoration work being carried out by the locals, who were painstakingly reinforcing the broken fragments of the sculptures. I stood there and watched them carry out their work. It was amazing how patiently and meticulously they were carrying out the restoration in bits and pieces!

I walked around the temple. There were 504 statues of Lord Buddha in the entire temple. Stone carvings were displayed everywhere. Over two million blocks of stone were assembled here during construction and over 3000 carvings engraved over the walls illustrated the teachings of life from Lord Buddha. Meticulously carved sculptures that started from the bottom level and went to the top methodically demonstrated the spiritual journey of life from the teaching of Lord Buddha. Magnificent! One must see it to believe it. This is supposedly the largest Buddha temple in the world and it is undoubtedly the pride of Indonesia. I wish I could have spent some more time going over the carvings in detail.

The temple was flooded with schoolchildren snapping photos here and there. They were mostly selfies. I suppose these tours were routinely organized or sponsored by the schools. I hoped the kids were learning some of the history behind the temple blended into every cornerstone. That would go so well with selfies. To my surprise, I hardly noticed any foreign tourists there that morning. I was pretty much the only foreigner with a backpack. So the students started taking my photos in their zeal to capture pictures. That was fine! I would not say 'no' to a photo-op as long as they were not mug shots, so I smiled for their photos. Slowly I covered eight levels of the temple and finally climbed up to the top. It was quite a climb. There were 72 dome-shaped stupas in the temple and at the apex of the temple sat the largest stupa which was the symbol of enlightenment.

I looked at my surroundings from the top and oh my God! It was a picture-perfect view of the landscape. The green hills of Java in the backdrop of the temple domes were like paintings on a canvas. This was a place to stand and ponder and history would open its pages. It will walk you through the forgotten path of history when the Sailendra dynasty once reigned in Java. Other than some sporadic cheers from students here and there or a couple chatting nearby, the atmosphere was serene and peaceful. Honestly, I was willing to sit down there all day and enjoy the serenity on my own. Too bad that I had a flight to catch in the late afternoon and I was yet to visit the Prambanan Temple. Damn! No, this was not a place that one should visit just as a tick mark on the bucket list, one must spend time here to appreciate its beauty and absorb the history. I wanted to spend much more time in such a historical place. But I had not planned it prudently. It was almost time for me to leave and I knew that I would regret it later.

I sighed and climbed down the stairs to the main level. The exit was on the other side of the main entrance. As expected, the exit took visitors through countless stalls of souvenirs where the sellers bugged you with all kinds of souvenirs ranging from T-shirts, baseball caps, small statues of the temple, Buddha statues and other items. You name it, they had it. I was familiar with this trick, so I zigzagged through the vendors and reached the main parking lot. There were hundreds of cars parked there.

"*Where the hell is my car*?" I thought and the fun began.

I had no idea where my driver had parked his car. I looked around but had no luck. I had zero knowledge of the parking lot and I hoped he was close by! Suddenly I recalled that he had given me his phone number, just in case. Unfortunately, sign language doesn't really work as audio. Oh well, it was worth a try because I didn't have much choice! I dialed his number and to my relief, I got through to him after a few rings. Then came the hard part. I managed to explain my location to him with great difficulty. After some challenging moments, he finally gave me his number plate.

"*That's progress*," I thought.

Unfortunately, the number turned out to be incorrect. I kept searching for the lot and calling him from time to time with growing frustration. Suddenly, I spotted him at a distance. He was sitting on a pillar near the car, looking pretty relaxed and unconcerned about my frustration. He saw me from a distance and waved his hand casually as if this was just a game of hide and seek. Indeed, it was no big deal but it was irritating. I was in no mood to argue with him about giving me the wrong number plate. And what should I argue about? How can you argue with someone when they cannot understand the language you speak? Long story short, I didn't make a fuss and we drove to our next destination, the Prambanan Temple.

The Prambanan Temple is actually a bit far from the Borobudur Temple. The latter lies in the northwest part of Yogyakarta while the Prambanan Temple is closer to its eastern portion. When the traffic is light, it takes slightly more than an hour to reach Prambanan from Borobudur. But if one is caught in the traffic, then it's anybody's guess. No wonder Desi had warned me that it wouldn't be easy to cover both temples in one day. She had suggested that I should spend an extra night in Jogja. Sometimes I become stubborn and prefer to go with my plan. I hadn't listened to her advice.

"*Serves me right!*" I thought.

I was checking my watch every minute or so, just in case I missed my flight! I was lucky that the traffic was light and I reached the temple in just about an hour. It was midday and there were hardly any tourists around! There was no line up at the ticket counter and no vendors were screaming to attract our attention. It was all very peaceful. I walked up to the counter and asked for one entrance ticket. Again, it was the same deal. I paid ten times more than a local would pay. Anyway, I had gotten used to this norm by then.

"*Well, it is what it is. Just suck it up,*" I told myself.

Earlier, in Borobudur, I had contemplated not visiting the temple in protest. That was just a silly, momentary knee-jerk reaction. Soon I came to my senses and decided that I had come all the way here to visit the famous temples that I always wanted to see. How could I call it quits just for extra 20 bucks? Was I stupid or what? This time, I quietly paid the entrance fee without making any fuss.

"Please stay here, don't go away," I told my driver with a hand gesture.

"Satu jam," the driver said in Bahasa and raised one finger.

I realized that he was asking me not to spend more than an hour inside the temple. I knew what was at stake, so I nodded and entered the temple complex.

As far as I know, Borobudur is the largest Buddhist temple in the world. Someone told me that Prambanan is the largest Hindu temple complex in the world. I am not totally sure about that. There are big Hindu temples in India and I thought that Angkor Wat was the largest Hindu temple in South East Asia. That said, some may argue whether Angkor Wat is a true Hindu temple or a fusion of Buddhism and Hinduism. No matter what, Prambanan was definitely the largest Hindu temple in Indonesia. It was built around the same time as Borobudur i.e. in the 9th century AD.

There were over 200 smaller temples inside the complex and three main temples. They were primarily dedicated to the Hindu trinity—Shiva, Vishnu and Brahma. Unlike Borobudur, there were scattered ruins of the temples inside the huge compound. Perhaps the Borobudur temple is more prominent and attracts a larger crowd than this one. But Prambanan is a beautiful temple complex and is a must-see while travelling to Yogyakarta. Like the Borobudur Temple, the Prambanan Temple Complex too is a UNESCO Heritage site and I could see some restoration work being carried out.

I didn't have much time to go around the entire complex at my own pace. But I visited the main temples and the corridors. The architecture there was definitely different from that in Borobudur and the deities were different too. I found that interesting! Given that the temple was built in the same era as the Sailendra Dynasty i.e. in the 9th century when the Borobudur Temple was built, two parallel streams of faith had coexisted in harmony. That speaks a lot about the diversity and openness of the empire in honouring various faiths. Something more surprising caught my attention when I started checking the smaller temples inside the complex. I saw the idol of the Indian Goddess Durga! Wow! I could understand the presence of the supreme trinity of the Hindu faith Shiva, Vishnu and Brahma that were displayed in a predominantly Hindu temple in Prambanan and elsewhere in Bali because they were the cornerstone of the Hindu religion. But Durga! That spoke about the depth of the Hindu mythology that had expanded to Indonesia from ancient India. Given that Prambanan was largely dedicated towards the Indian epic Ramayana, the presence of Devi Durga was a bit of a stretch. Actually, earlier I found that Ramayana had influenced local culture in Yogyakarta deeply. There were plays regularly shown in local theatres. This aspect was surely food for thought and I will leave it to my learned historians who can probably shed more light on it than I can.

It was already past 2 pm and I had a 4:30 pm flight to catch from Yogyakarta to Jakarta. I was hoping to beat the rush hour traffic and make it to the airport in time. I had calculated that if I could reach the airport in an hour, it would leave me with enough time for check-in and security. It was a pretty tight schedule! Given my earlier experience with Garuda Airlines, that actually narrowed the margin.

"Enough of temple hopping," I thought and hurried to the parking lot.

Thank God I didn't have to look around for my car this time. I jumped into the car and asked the driver to head out to the airport. Fortunately, he had been briefed on my itinerary. He didn't cause any delay and headed straight to the airport by zooming past the slower traffic.

On my way to the airport, I was thinking about the temples in Prambanan and Bali. Bali is rich in Hindu heritage and people there continue to practice their faith. I suppose the Prambanan Temple in Yogyakarta is more of a tourist attraction, an iconic symbol of ancient Hindu heritage. The manifestations are quite different in both places. As I said before, I am not a history buff, but I wish I had spent a bit more time there. But no regrets, I had always wanted to visit these temples. Even though it was a short trip, I was glad that I had made it. I was content that I had witnessed the footprints of history that spoke about an ancient era and a bygone civilization in Java.

Yogyakarta

At the entrance of
Borobudur Temple

Inside the Borobudur Temple

A view from the top of the temple

Prambanan Temple

Four:

Borneo – Call of wilderness

Borneo

A journey through the Wild West

The flight to Jakarta took off on time. No, I didn't miss my flight, but that was thanks to my lucky stars. God had smiled at me that day. We didn't face a lot of traffic on the way back to the airport and made it on time. But I am sure that unless I change my habit of travelling with such a back-to-back schedule, my luck will run out one of these days.

I looked out of my window seat as the aircraft landed in Jakarta's Soekarno-Hatta International Airport. The daylight was disappearing fast when we taxied to the terminal. Once the aircraft came to a complete halt and the seatbelt signs were turned off, I collected my backpack and stepped out. It was a nifty, tastefully designed airport with a modern terminal building. Jakarta is the most populous city in Indonesia. No, I didn't have any desire to spend time in Jakarta, at least not this time. To me, it was just another big city like many other cities in the world. The reason I had landed in Jakarta was because I had a connecting flight to Semarang that evening.

"What's in Semarang? Why travel there?" I had asked Desi when she had been working on my flight arrangements.

"You can get your connecting flight to Borneo from there," she told me.

I remember that I had made a lot of fuss about travelling to Borneo alone since I was concerned about my safety.

"Desi, is it safe to travel there alone? Can you fix me up with a group, please?" I insisted.

Things can go wrong, at the wrong place and wrong time. I knew that things had gone wrong for a lone traveller in Costa Rica just a few years ago.

Desi patiently listened to all my arguments and complaints and then told me, "Hey, it's not a typical tourist destination, you know."

"Come on, it's the orangutan's habitat and quite renowned. What are you talking about?"

"You see, I mostly get queries from the tourists coming to Bali. They travel to Bali, have fun, make a side trip to Ubud, visit some tourist attractions and go back home. I hardly get any tourists who want to spend time in the swamps in Borneo. No one wants to travel thousands of miles just to get some mosquito bites and get scared by crocs," she said bluntly.

"Is that a 'No'?"

"Not really, at least not yet. Ok, come over to Bali and let me see what I could do."

Then both she and Kadek told me the plan in detail over dinner in Bali. That was the night when I had arrived in Bali.

"My friend, we have a proposal to make," said Desi, starting the topic.

"I am listening," I said patiently.

I was also curious. I didn't have a clue as to what she had in her mind.

"You see, we are from Bali. We have hardly visited the west coast. Would you mind if we come along with you?"

I couldn't believe my ears at first. Desi and Kadek were both smiling and I stared at them, wide-eyed. I had won the jackpot! Who on earth would believe that my tour organizer and her boyfriend would join me on my dream trip?

"You are kidding, right?" I said as I still couldn't believe it!

"No, we are not. We would like to join you if you don't mind. And we will share the cost—fifty-fifty! Deal?"

My jaws dropped! Was I hearing this right? I straightened myself on the chair, shook my head a few times in disbelief and finally told her, "I can't believe it! Are you sure?"

They were still smiling.

"Yes, we are," she replied.

I was over the moon. I almost screamed, "What are you waiting for? Go pack your bags!"

Yes, that was exactly what I had told them. I don't know how this always happens to me. I recalled my trip to Thailand. I was searching for a reliable tour guide who could arrange a road trip to Mae Hong Son for me. It was a faraway, non-descriptive sleepy border town near Myanmar. But I couldn't find anyone who would agree to take me there.

"Where, Mae Hong Son? Sorry, Sir, we cannot do it," was the standard reply.

Finally, when I had almost given up hope, my luck opened up. That is when I found Oppy and Alex, tour organizers from Chiang Mai in Thailand. I asked Alex if he would be able to arrange a tour for me to Mae Hong Son.

"Why do you want to go there? There is nothing to see," Alex told me.

"Exactly the reason why," I replied.

"You know there are over 1800 mountain passes you have to cross to reach Mae Hong Son! It's not easy to drive up there," Alex told me flatly.

"Well Alex, anything difficult excites me. And you know, I stay away from the normal tourist spots. I love to travel to no-name places."

I had almost given up hope. He seemed just like the other guides. Alex thought for a moment and then spread his hands in despair.

"You know, you are crazy," he sighed and finally agreed to drive me up there.

Then he said, "Okay, I will take you there, but on one condition. My girlfriend Oppy comes with me."

"Even better! Party time!"

"I'm serious. I know you will be flying out from Mae Hong Son. What about me? I refuse to drive back alone on that road. No way," said Alex, frowning at me.

"It's a deal!"

"Expense is all yours," said Alex bluntly.

"Did I say 'No'?"

"Ok boss, done."

And it was done. Boy oh boy, we had so much fun on the road! Even today, whenever we chat about that trip, Oppy always says it was a trip of a lifetime. Now it was happening again! It was the same deal but this time it was with Desi and Kadek. A trip to Borneo with me! Dreams do come true! Not only that, a cost-sharing proposal was on the table! What else could I ask for? Boy oh boy!

"What are you thinking?" Desi asked me.

"Umm, no, nothing, I was just roaming through my past years," I said and laughed.

The sequence of events in both cases was so similar that it caught me by surprise.

We finished our dinner, but I wanted to discuss it some more.

So, I began seriously, "Ok, let's talk logistics."

"Meaning?"

"I am leaving Bali to travel to Komodo island. Desi, you know my flight details. Where are we meeting then? And when?"

"We meet in Semarang."

"Semarang? Really?"

"Yup, you are flying from Jogja to Semarang via Jakarta to catch your flight to Pangkalan Ban, Borneo, ok?"

"That's what you arranged for me. Yes, I get it."

"Kadek and I fly to Semarang from Bali and meet you there. Then we will all fly together from Semarang to Borneo, got it?"

It seemed like Desi had already chalked out the plan.

"And then? How long do we stay in Borneo?"

"Two nights. Once we are done, Kadek and I will go back to Bali and you head out to Surabaya, got it?"

"Hang on. What happens if I say 'No'?" I couldn't stop myself from joking to see her reaction.

"Then you date the crocs on your own in the swamp of Borneo. We are done! Hahaha," Desi laughed loudly.

"Deal!"

"Deal and high five! See you in Semarang then," Desi was all smiles.

That is the reason why I flew to Semarang. While I waited for my luggage at Semarang airport, I thought about my chat with Desi and Kadek that evening and laughed. No matter how much I enjoy exploring a new place, it's always exciting when I have company, especially in places like Borneo with deep jungles and swamps. First, it would be totally safe to have friends around. Second, I wouldn't be lonely during the whole trip. And let's face it, having to deal with locals with my language barrier wouldn't be that easy. I recalled my car driver in Yogyakarta! I was sure that the poor guy was happy to finally drop me off at the airport on time. So this was great! On top of it, both Desi and Kadek are fun-loving guys and we would be sharing our fun. That would be icing on the cake for sure! So I was sure that it would be an exciting journey to Borneo. Usually, I get a bit tense when I travel to a new place and stay alert. But now I could let my guard down a bit, because not only did I have a couple of good friends, but they were also locals from Indonesia. Suddenly, I felt at home in Semarang.

When I came out of the terminal, I looked for my prearranged taxi but not for long. The cabbie was there with my name tag and he spoke English. What a relief! We hit the road and I kept looking around to check the city out as we drove to the hotel. Though it was nighttime, I liked Semarang from whatever I could see. It was nifty, newer than Jogja and appeared to be a planned city. The roads were wide and the broad dividers had trees and flowers planted in them. The neon-lit roads were nice and bright. The traffic appeared to be lighter than in Bali and Yogyakarta. The Amaris hotel was not too far from the airport and I thanked the driver once we reached there. I reminded him that he needed to pick us up early in the morning. He nodded and drove away. I headed toward the reception. It was a budget hotel but a decent one. The folks in the reception were cordial and assigned me a room on the fifth floor. It was an ordinary room, but good enough for a night's stay. There was no restaurant inside the hotel, just a cafeteria which was closed at that hour. I was glad that I had grabbed a sandwich from the Jakarta airport and I was set for the night.

First things first! I called Desi after freshening up. They had already checked in. Their room was on the third floor. So I hurriedly climbed down two flights of stairs and knocked on their door. Kadek opened it and I screamed and jumped for joy. We had dinner together just a few days back in Sanur, but it felt like I was meeting them after years!

"Yay, you made it," said Desi and came running. It was time for a bear hug and our reunion.

"The room is very small, so please don't mind!" said Kadek, apologetically.

"Who cares? We are together, and that's all it matters bud! Besides, we are here just for a night, so cut it out, man!"

I was beaming with excitement. I realized that Kadek and Desi wanted to finish packing so I left them to do that after we chatted for a while. It was too early to go to bed, so I decided to take a walk down the streets just to check the city out. I do that for all the new places that I visit. Who knows if I will be here again in the future? So why not?

The next day, it was an early morning run for all three of us. The flight was to leave at 8:25 am and we wanted to grab breakfast quickly before heading out to the airport. The cafeteria was open, so a mug of coffee and a hasty breakfast of toast and fried eggs was perfect. The taxi was waiting for us, so we quickly checked out and headed straight to the airport.

Was I excited? Boy oh boy! Actually, that would be an understatement. I was overjoyed! It was the trip of a lifetime and a trip that I had been dreaming about for years. And finally, things had fallen into place and it was going to happen! Not only that, but it was also all arranged perfectly, like ducks in a row. We all boarded the Kalstar flight in a cheerful mood. It was a small propeller-driven plane with two seats on each side of the aisle. Once we settled down, the flight took off after a short run. I looked out the window. As we were climbing up, I could see my short-lived 'city of joy' Semarang fading away behind the clouds in the grey morning! I sighed and leaned back in my seat. We smiled at each other and relaxed for our next destination, Borneo!

Borneo – my childhood dream

When I was a little boy growing up in India, I remember the monsoon days when I used to cuddle up to my father in the evenings and pester him to tell me stories about the jungles around the world, about the tigers, the lions and other animals. My father was an awesome storyteller. He used to tell me the stories of Jim Corbett and the man-eating tigers, lions in Africa, dense forests in Borneo and his own experiences in the jungles in India. Curled up next to him, I used to listen to those amazing stories as it rained outside. With the symphony of torrential rains on the tin roof, I used to roam around in a make-believe world of the animal kingdom in my childhood dreams, from the vast savannas of Africa to the dense forests of Borneo. Slowly, I used to drift into my fantasy world and go to sleep. So many years have passed since then, but whenever I walk down memory lane, I remember my childhood dreams. I realized that my dreams were still alive and my desire to travel to Borneo had never died.

The Kalstar flight from Semarang landed in Pangkalan Bun in Central Borneo after an hour. It was a cloudy morning in December. We were all excited and wanted to start the day early. We knew that we had a long boat ride sailing on the Kumai river ahead of us before we could trek in the jungle to spot orangutans.

Pangkalan Bun was a sleepy town with a sizeable population making their livelihood mostly from fishing in the Kumai river. The road leaving from the airport to the town was pretty much empty. The big leafy trees on both sides of the road were swaying under a grey sky. It was a quiet ride on the cloudy morning and I fell in love with the town at first sight. There was no chaos, no crowd, no dazzling shopping market other than a half-empty Borneo mall and hardly any traffic on the road. I loved it! Desi and Kadek who lived in the tourist haven of Bali were not used to this quiet, but they loved it here too.

Adventure Indonesia, where Desi used to work, has a small branch in Pangkalan Bun and we needed to visit their local outlet first to pick up our guide and the crew members for the boat. Once there, it didn't take us long as the crew was ready. We picked them up and headed out to the boat waiting for us on the Kumai river.

Borneo is split into two parts which fall into two different countries. The smaller one is a part of Malaysia and is known as Kota Kinabalu. The larger part is known as Kalimantan and its vast land, forests and watercourse are a part of Indonesia. I had never been to Kota Kinabalu, but I heard that the place is very nicely arranged for tourists. It is a well-organized and comfortable resort. Efficient group tours specialized in trekking for orangutans are also available. Perhaps it is easier for travellers on a tight schedule but it was not my cup of tea. Adventure and risk-taking are in my blood. I am never content with 'made for you' solutions when I travel in the outback. I really wanted to travel and trek in the natural habitat of orangutans and experience the unspoiled wilderness. I wanted to visit the jungles of Kalimantan. My childhood images of Borneo were very much alive in my mind.

My initial plan before coming here was to reach Balikpapan in East Kalimantan and then take a boat to travel along the Mahakam river. This mighty river runs close to 1000 km through the vast wilderness of Borneo. I was planning to stop at riverside villages from time to time, meet the Dayak tribes and trek through the jungles to catch the boat at its next stop. But I gathered that the plan would require a minimum of seven days which I couldn't afford. I was willing to give it three days maximum. I decided to keep Mahakam for another day and started looking for alternatives and found this one.

I had read about the anthropologist Dr. Biruté Mary Galdikas, a Toronto-born scientist with a Lithuanian background. Dr. Galdikas had travelled to Tanjung Puting Reserve in Central Borneo in 1971 to study the orangutans. This motivated and dedicated scientist was determined to study the orangutans in their natural habitat. Dr. Galdikas persuaded her US-based guide Dr. Leakey to fund this project. After facing several odds, she finally succeeded in setting foot in the swamps of central Borneo. There were no roads, no electricity, no TV, only endless swamps filled with crocs, snakes, mosquitoes and spiders. You name it, the swamps had it.

People told her, "Don't go! Orangutans are too elusive and the place is too dangerous to survive."

Did she listen? Of course not! That was the start of her illustrious career. She spent 40 years of her life studying orangutans and established Camp Leakey in Tanjung Putting across the jungles and backwater swamps spanning hundreds of kilometres. Today, undoubtedly, she is an authority on the life and behaviour of orangutans. During her career, she has received many prestigious awards and continues to call Indonesia her home. Tanjung Putting is a national park and the credit for preserving the ecosystem here goes to her. In her passion, I saw the reflection of Dian Fossey who gave her life in Rwanda while pursuing her dream of saving the gorillas from being poached.

This appeared to be a good alternative for me. With this plan, I could still pursue my dream of travelling to Borneo and trekking to see orangutans. As a bonus, I could visit Camp Leakey, the wonderful creation of a dedicated scientist. To be honest, it would be my way of offering a little tribute to her life and her legendary work.

"Desi, where are we going to stay at night when in Borneo?" I asked her.

"You have two options. You could stay at Rimba Lodge but it would cost you more," she replied.

"And what is the second option?" I asked.

"Spend the night in a klotok, a wooden boat. It's cheaper."

Desi told me that the lodge was away from civilization and nestled in the forest and the swamp. It was a nice place with all the comforts of a hotel. But I didn't want that. I wanted to experience the nightlife in the middle of total wilderness. A klotok would be ideal for that. So I decided on that for the two nights instead of a comfortable lodge.

"Would you and Kadek be okay to spend the night on a klotok?" I asked hesitantly.

Desi gave her lovely smile, looked at Kadek and nodded, "We would love it, wouldn't we?"

She had her arm laced around Kadek's neck.

"But one thing," she continued.

"What is it?"

"I would like to check out the Rimba Lodge sometime during our trip. You know, for future marketing purposes."

"Got it! Not an issue. Done," I told her.

The Kumai river is very wide near the township of Pangkalan Bun. It was around midday when we started our boat journey. We sailed along the river for over an hour until the river joined the Sekonyer river. Soon, the landscape started to change. The fishing villages on both sides of the Kumai river we saw when we started were long gone. The river started narrowing down, finally joining the Sekonyer river and then turning into a large canal. The river now flowed through the marshland and excess water from the river spread across the lowland and created large backwater swamps stretching deep within the wetland. Both sides of the river were packed with palm trees, grassland and swamps.

Beyond the swamps, there was a dense forest. Tall trees created darkness underneath them even in the daylight. What type of wildlife lived there and in how many numbers was anybody's guess. We saw some proboscis monkeys on the tree tops, but no orangutans. They are usually elusive. The river water was dark and had turned muddy by then. While observing the river and backwaters from the boat, I caught a glimpse of a snake swimming through the river towards the grassy swamp. It's hard to say how far within the land the swamp ran. It reminded me of my journey to Tortuguero in Costa Rica. Tortuguero is surrounded by water bodies and the only way to reach it is either by boat or by air. We were travelling to Torteguero from the capital San Jose by boat. Just like the Kumai river, backwaters from the rivers in Tortuguero often stretched deep within the grassland.

I asked the boat captain, "How far do the swamps run inside?"

"Hard to say, maybe a mile or two," he replied.

"Do people go trekking inside?" I was itching to find out as I loved hiking in the wilderness.

"Oh yeah, some go but they never come back," he replied flatly, keeping his hands on the steering wheel.

Still, I had tried trekking for a night inside the swamps in Costa Rica with a guide. I must say, it was fun! The swamps on both sides of the Sekonyer river reminded me of what the captain told me and I shuddered. I wondered how Dr. Galdikas managed to live here day in and day out. I didn't think I could survive.

Our guide told us that one side of the Sekonyer river was leased by the industries making palm oil from the palm trees and the other side was a part of the National Park, stretching over hundreds of square miles. There was a constant effort from Dr. Galdikas to preserve the area as a habitat for the orangutans. As I said, I was awed whenever I thought about how a person could live and work in this swamp surrounded by dense tropical forest day after day. It was not only difficult but also extremely dangerous. Crocs can ambush one in the swamps and red ants can slowly creep out from their hidden mounds and can eat you alive if you take one wrong step. God alone knows what kind of snakes and other types of creatures were out there to hunt you down. Undaunted, Dr. Galdikas made friends with the orangutans and took care of them. I don't think they gave her a warm welcome when she first arrived here! I was amazed at the intense dedication and motivation that can drive a person to live through this. I bowed my head out of respect for her.

It was noon and I was hungry! I had just eaten a croissant and had coffee before boarding my early morning flight from Semarang.

"Hey Desi, any idea when we can get some food?" I knew Desi would have the information. After all, she had arranged the tour.

"Hold your horses, don't worry. The crew will bring it over here soon."

There was a small round table at one side and we waited patiently until they brought the platters. Oh my! I drooled when lunch was served. Steamed rice, beans with mixed vegetables, fried eggplants and cooked fish with large prawns on the side! It was a gourmet meal! It was definitely beyond my expectations. I had not thought that such an elegant platter could be served at lunchtime in the middle of nowhere. It reminded me of the fantastic meals that the crew had served us when I travelled to Komodo island. Perhaps, this is the Indonesian tradition of hospitality or it could be the magic wand used by our queen Ms. Desi Yanti. Whatever the reason it was, I was thankful!

"Happy now?" Desi grinned.

After all, she felt proud of this service from her company and rightly so! I returned her smile and dived into the food. I am not a big lunch eater, usually, just a sandwich is good enough for me at lunchtime. But the word 'usually' is a disclaimer. I am not a fool to turn down such a great meal, especially when I was hungry! Oh, I must point out that, generally, people in Indonesia are fond of eating rice. I had observed that it was usually included in most of their meals, similar to the eating habits in some Indian states.

The Sekonyer river has turned into just a narrow canal by then, with grassland spread everywhere on the river bank. The boat was sailing downstream slowly through the canal. I sat on the starboard and was absorbing the beauty of the wilderness. It was a different world out there, quite different from the rain forest in Costa Rica or the dry savannah in Africa. The river was muddy at that point. The backwater had penetrated inside the dense foliage on both sides and tall trees often interlaced with each other preventing the entry of sunlight. I couldn't see or hear any birds and there was an eerie silence all around us, except for the humming of the engine. That was an uncanny feeling. I was sure that we were being watched and without knowing what kind of wildlife was living inside the dense jungle, I certainly felt that the boat was our ultimate sanctuary. The more I saw, the more I was amazed and wondered about how Dr. Galdikas managed to survive in this no man's land. It was no cakewalk, it was dangerous. Surely the brave soul had put her own life in danger while pursuing her dream. Hats off to her! Such people are the ones who can make a difference in this world.

We reached the 'Pondok Tangui Rehab Center' early in the afternoon. This part of Tanjung Puting was designed for the orangutan. We were lucky there was no rain when we arrived. Usually, that part of the world received heavy rain, especially in the rainy season which was in November-December. Actually, Indonesia practically has two seasons, wet and dry. Most parts of Indonesia get a heavy dose of rainfall throughout the year, more often during the rainy season. Our boat slowly came to a stop and anchored next to a wooden boardwalk that ran over the swamp up to a certain point. Then there was a pathway that ran through the fairly dense wooded areas which were not easy to navigate. We started our trek and Desi and Kadek walked ahead with the guide navigating through the rough patches. Often, the trail was waterlogged and we had to take detours. Sometimes, we didn't even have the luxury to detour. We had to slowly walk on some makeshift rickety puncheon bridges made from tree trunks. If anyone has tried it before, they know for sure that it's not easy to walk over round tree trunks. We had to maintain our balance constantly. A couple of times we slipped into the water below. Fortunately, it was not deep and only our shoes got wet. I remember when we trekked in a swamp in Costa Rica, we were wearing rubber boots supplied by the lodge where we stayed. There it was at night and sometimes we walked in ankle-deep water. Here too, I wished we were wearing rubber boots while trekking over these areas. Fortunately, the guide knew the area well and his eyes scanned the surroundings as we walked. Since he was ahead of us, sometimes he warned us well in advance. Once he suddenly stopped and turned around. We stopped walking too.

He pointed towards a large ant mound on the trail and said, "Make sure you don't step on it."

We hadn't noticed it. Deadly red ants swarmed the place. I hadn't seen such large red ants in my life before. Each one was almost the size of a mid-sized spider. If we had not been warned, we would have stepped into the mound. I don't want to think about what would have happened next. And mosquitoes! Oh boy! If we had not carried the mosquito repellents with us, they would have eaten us alive.

We were trekking to witness the orangutans at a feeding point in Tanjung Putin National Park. It was not easy, but we finally made it and that too on time. The timing was perfect as the volunteers were getting ready to feed the orangutans. A rectangular table was placed in a small opening inside the woods and a couple of people from the camp dumped a sack full of bananas. Then they started calling the orangutans by sending out a high pitch message that sounded like 'Uk Uk Uk.' We searched the dense canopy of trees, but couldn't see any movement at first. We waited for nearly twenty minutes before they started appearing one by one on the treetops. Soon there were around ten to fifteen of them hanging from the trees. Then they slowly came down one by one. We were surprised to see that they were not in a hurry. They didn't scramble down the trees in chaos to get to the bananas but arrived in an orderly fashion. The group seemed to have some kind of hierarchy in their social system.

We watched a large male orangutan arrive first. He consumed quite a few of the bananas while the others waited for him to finish his lunch. Once he was done, he grabbed a mouthful of bananas, climbed up the trees and disappeared. Then the rest of them climbed down one at a time and grabbed their share. They didn't fight or snatch food from one another. They collected their share calmly. I was not sure if they had been trained to do so, but it was quite a show! A female came down with a child clinging to her and she placed a handful of bananas in her mouth. She looked around, grabbed some more bananas in one hand and climbed up the tree using the other free hand. Then she jumped from one tree top to another with the bananas in her mouth still holding the baby. I was amazed at the strength of her arms.

Suddenly it started raining. As the water dripped down from the leaves, the orangutans disappeared. Our guide told us that the orangutans did not like rain. Ironically, Borneo is a tropical rainforest. Rainfall is a part of life here. I was wondering whether the orangutans had chosen the wrong place as their permanent habitat! On our part, we were prepared for the rain as we were carrying our 'ponchos.' This was thanks to Desi who had reminded me to bring them several times before the trip. But my running shoes were soaking wet from my earlier slips. Even though I could manage that, the mosquitoes were the most irritating. They were merciless and thank God we had an ample supply of the repellant. We also helped some other tourists to save them from the bites. Anyway, it was the end of the show as the rain started pouring in and we headed back to the boat. It was a fair bit of a hike and by the time we returned to our boat, we were all soaked.

The upper floor of the boat was reserved for us. On one side there were three mattresses for us to sleep on. On the starboard side, a small dining table was placed. We used to hang around there when not trekking in the woods. I removed my wet running shoes once we came back from the trek and left them in a corner to dry. I didn't have a choice, as I did not have a second pair. To be honest, I didn't expect to slip into the water, but I should have been better prepared. Anyway, I had learnt my lesson.

Still, there was plenty of daylight and it was not time for supper yet, so I decided to climb up to the upper deck.

"What are you up to?" Desi asked me as I climbed up the stairs.

"Well, it's not time for supper yet and I want to get a good view of the jungles from the top."

"We will join you," said Desi and she and Kadek got up right away.

We carried our cameras and climbed up to the upper deck. I realized that the captain's cabin was blocking our view in the front. There was a small stool nearby and I climbed up to the cabin's roof using the stool. It was probably kept there for the crew for the same purpose. Once settled, I looked around. The view from the roof was fantastic! No, it was not a view of majestic mountains or a landscape with picturesque rolling hills or a scenic river view. It was nothing like that. The Sekonyer river was just a narrow canal here with red muddy water and swampy grassland covering both sides of the river. Beyond the grassland were dense palm trees. It was late afternoon. The grey sky was slowly turning dark with the sun going down the horizon. With looming darkness, there was eerie silence everywhere. It seemed as if we were the only living creatures in the world. Even the daylight could not penetrate the foliage. I could not spot a single bird anywhere. A couple of proboscis monkeys were eyeing our boat from the top of the tall trees as if they were keeping an eye from the watch tower.

The overhanging grasslands were so close that I could even touch them if our boat was a bit closer. I could feel that danger was lurking just around the corner—just one wrong step and we would be done! I shivered and those were the times when I felt that the boat was my only shelter. Truly, it was uncanny. There was no sound except the humming noise of the engine and that sounded even louder in the quietness all around us. Kadek and I set our videos in time-lapse mode to capture the gradual changes in the landscape which seemed to stretch for miles.

"Do you like it?" asked Desi.

I turned around. I didn't know when Desi quietly came up to join us.

"I just love it. What about you?" I looked at her.

"Same," she answered while looking at the densely wooded area.

"Any regrets about joining me?"

"Well, I was the one who proposed that we join the trip, isn't it?" she looked at me and smiled, then continued, "You see, we never get to see this when in Bali or Ubud or anywhere else close by!"

"What about Irian Jaya, the West Papua? That's not too far from Bali."

"Well, that's a different world, you know. Besides, I wanted to see this part of my country. I love it!" she said contentedly.

"I am still missing another part," I said.

"Where is that?"

"Sumatra. Perhaps another time."

"You are squeezing too many things in one go. Sometimes you have to contemplate and appreciate. You should not make a habit of touch and go. It's not a checklist, you know," she said while gazing at the horizon.

"I suppose you are right. I have put Sumatra on my bucket list, for the future.

It was getting dark and we had had a long day. So we climbed down the ladder and relaxed a bit. Desi and Kadek took a shower but not me. I like to take a shower in the morning. The crew had already closed the windows to stop the insects from the swamp from coming inside. They get attracted by the lights. Besides, if we had not closed the windows, the mosquitoes would have had a party time.

A steaming hot dinner was served as I just started getting hungry. The menu made me even hungrier. It was steamed rice with mixed vegetables, fried prawns and salad on the side! I thoroughly enjoyed it. Once we were done, we chatted for a while. It was dark outside and there was nothing much to do. Also, we were all tired from the day's hike. Desi and Kadek called it a night and Desi fixed the mosquito net over the mattresses. Oh yes, one needed a mosquito net here for sleeping at night. Otherwise, the mosquitoes would perhaps drag you into the swamp. The guide also warned us not to open the windows at night.

"Why is that?" I asked.

He gave me a look and said, "You never know."

Then he disappeared to his room downstairs.

Hmmm, we looked at each other. I wondered what kind of beast would try to get inside through the windows at night!

"Whatever," I shrugged.

"Good night," said Desi.

She and Kadek were already inside the mosquito net and were settling on their pillows.

She asked me, "What are you up to?"

"Climbing to the deck, just want to enjoy the darkness, you know."

"Don't fall for a croc!" she laughed.

"Good night!" I said, turned off the light and climbed up to the deck.

I took a chair and sat down in complete darkness. Mosquitoes were swirling everywhere. Thank God I carried my mosquito repellant. The boat was anchored in a swamp near grassy land. I could hear the crew talking downstairs and the sound of utensils. After a while it all became quiet and the lights were turned off. I checked my watch. It was around 9 pm. In this part of the world, especially in the swamp and dense forest, that was a late hour. I was listening to Simon Garfunkel's '*Hello darkness my old friend*' on MP3. It was my favourite song. I turned off the player once the song was done. No, this was not the right time to listen to the music. Spending a night in this swamp was unique, I would not experience this again. This is why I had come here. It was special. I wanted to absorb the night alone on my own, deep inside my heart. This was mine, totally mine!

As the late evening turned into night, the sound of creatures in the woods and swamps around me became louder. Hundreds of creatures woke up and informed the world that they were alive. A night bird was chirping "ti-ti-ti" non-stop as if it was telling the world, "Don't forget me, I'm here." As long as I was sitting there, it did not stop. The whole swamp and the jungle around me came to life more than they had been during the daytime.

"*Where the hell were they all this time?*" I wondered quietly.

It was pitch dark and the rest of the world had gone to sleep. I slowly drifted into this world of darkness, its obscurity, though vibrant with the rhythmic sound of the nighttime concert all around me. I felt it in every molecule of my very existence. Yes, I came to Borneo just for this and no, I wouldn't have got this experience in my urban life where the cacophony of hundreds of car engines filled up my daily routine. I sat there motionless. The wild darkness was creeping into my vein and my soul.

While sitting there in a trance, someone whispered the eternal truth in my ear, "*Life is not a dress rehearsal, this is it.*" So go and enjoy the moments and embrace the wilderness!

Yes, I was in a complete trance with the symphony of the night concert ringing in my head. When I opened my eyes, it was past midnight! I got out of my chair and climbed down the stairs.

"Tomorrow is another day," I told myself and crawled inside my bed. Kadek and Desi were fast asleep!

I woke up early like I always do. A few hours of sleep at night is good enough for me and that works well whenever I travel. Mornings are always calm and peaceful. That is the time when I like to take a deep breath to feel the start of a new day. I checked my watch. It was almost five in the morning. The two lovebirds were still fast asleep, so I did not disturb them. After washing my face, I climbed up to the deck. Daylight was just breaking out from behind a cloudy sky and I could hear some birds busy with their daily chores. I hadn't heard many birds the day before on our way there. A pristine and peaceful early morning embraced me with love. A morning mist hovered over the mangroves in the swamp. All creatures of the night had gone to sleep and an eerie calm blanketed the misty wilderness.

"*Today is my last day in Borneo, so take it all,*" I told myself.

I knew these would be memories that would last for the rest of my life. What else do we need?

"*Take only memories, leave only footprints,*" I whispered.

Oh yes, we were yet to see Camp Leakey and I was also keen on visiting a local village. I was toying with that idea and mentioned it to our guide when

I was alone with him. He told me that we would pass Sekonyer village on our way back from Camp Leakey. So I expressed my interest in visiting the place as it would probably be a once in a lifetime opportunity for me to meet the locals and learn about their lifestyle. What do they do? And how do they survive living so far away from civilization?

When we were walking back to the boat the previous day, I had asked Desi, "Would you guys like to see a local village? I would like to."

Desi looked at Kadek, then said, "I'm game. But I wouldn't mind having a quick look at Rimba Lodge first."

Oh yes, Rimba Lodge! Desi had mentioned that to me earlier.

I was in a lighter mood. So I joked and giggled, "Oh, I see! You are planning to shift there tonight, Desi, aren't you? Didn't you like our company on the boat?"

"Haha, funny! No, it's business, my friend, like I told you before. I may have to recommend the lodge to my clients in the future. It helps when I see it with my own eyes."

"Sure, by all means. I know, you told me. I was just kidding."

Then I turned to the guide and asked, "How are we doing with time?"

"We will make it," the guide nodded while gazing outside. So I knew it was settled.

Well, our agenda was totally full for the day—Camp Leakey, Rimba Lodge, and visiting a local village. The six-cylinder engine of the boat roared into life around 7 am. Desi and Kadek were up and we had our breakfast—toast with scrambled eggs, orange juice, bananas and of course, a pot of coffee to go with it. When there is nothing else around us other than miles of swamp and dense forest, food becomes a part-time occupation and perhaps it tastes better while we enjoy the beauty of wilderness all around us. But I must admit, the food was fantastic all through this trip and the items were tastefully chosen by our chef. We hung around the dining table chatting and taking photos well after breakfast while the boat sailed through the murky river. A second round of coffee was served to us and that suited our mood just fine.

We anchored near Camp Leakey around 10 am. This place had more traffic than Tanjung Putting. There were other boats with loads of tourists anchored nearby. We jumped out of the boat onto the boardwalk. My running shoes were mostly dry and walking along the pathway was much easier here than at Tanjung Putting. We walked for some time through the wooded areas till we came to a small courtyard with a few cabins. This is where Dr. Galdikas used to spend her days while pursuing her dream. There was a small building near the cabins. The guide told us that it was specially built for the rehabilitation of orangutans.

"Ok, let's check it out," I told Desi as I led them to the entrance of the building.

There was a moderately-sized lobby which had been used as a rehab camp for orangutans in the past. The lobby had been converted into a museum showcasing the history of the camp. Many photographs were on display showing the orangutans with Dr. Galdikas and her staff during various phases of rehab. The items used by her were also on display. The photos on the wall provided a detailed history of the camp. The feeding time was around noon and we still had plenty of time to spend. We walked around the hall viewing the displays and photographs. One of the photos caught my attention. It displayed the cover page of an old TIME magazine. The cover page showed Dr. Galdikas holding the hand of an orangutan while another baby orangutan clung to her like a baby clings to its mother. It was a landmark recognition of a passionate and motivated scientist who made a difference in this obscure part of the world. She didn't do it for publicity or fame, she did it for her passion to save a species from extinction. It was right from her heart. There was no showing off, no pretence.

Dedicated people like her and Dian Fossey are rare. Just across from the museum was the small cabin where the doctor used to live her simple life. It was just a plain cabin with basic amenities, surrounded by deep woods and swamps. There was no security as such. No security from the wilderness and none from the corporate world. After all, her crusade to create a sanctuary for the orangutans was against the vested interest of the palm oil industry which wanted to occupy the land on both sides of the Sekonyer river. Dr. Galdikas fought relentlessly against the industry to restrict their vast empire to one side of the river only. She thus saved the land from deforestation while creating the habitat. I was told that she still lives in Indonesia, a country she made her home. Apparently, she is well-respected in Indonesia and the government values her advice, which is truly commendable.

"It's show time," whispered Desi as we neared the feeding spot for the orangutans.

It was a bit of a walk through the dense bushes of ferns and other natural growth. We reached the feeding area but again there was no sign of them! The area was more well organized compared to Tanjung Putting. There were some benches for the visitors. We sat down and waited. The opening was surrounded by tall trees and bushes. The place was, of course, infested with mosquitoes. My mosquito repellant bottle was already half empty from constant use. Suddenly I felt water droplets on my arm. I looked up and saw that it had started raining. I covered my camera with my poncho and looked at where Desi and Kadek were sitting.

"Thank you for the ponchos, Desi."

I was really thankful as it was her idea. She winked at me.

Fortunately, it was not a downpour but a drizzle. Then the volunteers came and dumped sacks of bananas on the bench as usual. The volunteers started calling the orangutans but they didn't show up. I knew orangutans don't like rain, but it had stopped by then. We waited and waited and I had almost given up when we noticed that the tops of the forty-foot-high trees had started shaking. Then they came, one by one, almost 15 of them including the children clinging to their mothers.

As we had seen in Tanjung Putin, a big guy, possibly the group leader climbed down first. He looked around and started gobbling as many bananas as he could. Unlike the leader whom we had seen earlier in Tanjung Putin, this guy seemed to be in a hurry. He seemed to be anxious to finish his bananas. The way he was constantly glancing over his shoulder while eating the bananas showed his concern. I figured that he was probably not the group leader but the deputy. Finally, he grabbed a handful of bananas, pushed them in his mouth as quickly as he could and hurriedly climbed up a tree and disappeared. We never found out who the group leader was. I looked up to my right and a younger one was casually hanging from a tree branch just over our head in a display of mockery, I suppose.

Most of the bananas disappeared in a short time and so did the orangutans. The rain had stopped and we started on our way back to the boat. But we didn't follow in the footsteps of the other visitors. Our guide made a detour and took a shortcut through the dense, tall trees around us. Just as we started, I heard a sudden rustling in the trees. We stopped and looked up. I saw an orangutan high above us. It then jumped from one tree top to another.

At first, we thought, "Oh yes, it was their natural habitat and it was quite normal that they were jumping around."

So we didn't pay much attention and continued to walk. Soon we realized that the animal was indeed stalking us. I couldn't read its mind, but I was in no mood to start a brawl with one of them knowing very well that they were in the majority there. If I touch one of them, probably ten will come from nowhere to pounce on me. Besides, I had earlier seen how strong their arms were. Just one slap and I wouldn't stand a chance. So we hurried to get out of the dense wood. We came to a relatively open area and I was relieved, only to find out that the orangutan was ahead of us.

"*Oh, no!*" I murmured.

She possibly knew a better way to outrun us. I learned later from the locals that her name was 'Siswi.' The boat crews who were regular here actually know Siswi very well. She waited for us on a tree until we crossed her. As soon we passed her, she jumped down to the boardwalk from the tree. I glanced over my shoulder and saw that she was patiently stalking us. Probably it was her regular game with the tourists. By that time other visitors had joined us on the boardwalk. Siswi passed us and walked close to a boat. I started following her keeping a safe distance. She glanced over her shoulder and looked straight into my eyes... just like another human being. What an intense look! It looked as if she was reading my mind! I waited until she glanced in another direction. Slowly, I went close to her. She gave me another look and then shooed me with one arm! It was quite obvious that she didn't like me! What had I done to her? Perhaps she thought I was a threat!

Perhaps she had ignored me since she thought, "*Oh, just another paparazzi, go away.*"

That's fine, I had been rejected in the past, although not by an orangutan, and that was ok... I was used to it! Besides, I didn't even belong to her clan, so she had every reason to dismiss me. Well, wait a minute. Wait till you listen to this and you can judge her yourself! I was standing close to Siswi when a lady walked by. Siswi looked at her and did not shoo her or react negatively! She just accepted her presence and greeted her in a friendly manner! Well, was that fair? Yeah right, my hairline had thinned just like Siswi's bald head and I am no Clint Eastwood either! So she dumped me without a second thought! But she didn't have any issue with another woman! Damn it, that was clearly discrimination!

Apparently, Siswi was known for hanging out at the anchor area for food and drinks, although tourists were forbidden to feed the animals. While I was standing there fuming about her behaviour, Siswi dived into a parked boat, went inside the pilot's cabin and came out with a mug half filled with Coca-Cola! To my surprise, she started drinking and relishing it!

"*Total brat,*" I thought.

At least she could have shown some manners in front of the people who had come all this way to see her here! No manners, no gender neutrality and obvious bias! Nha, I didn't have time for this impolite and prejudiced orangutan, I too decided to dump her and boarded my boat. Yeah, the feeling was quite mutual!

Our main mission was done. We had trekked to view orangutans and to witness the legacy created by Dr. Galdikas. This meant a lot to me. I had indeed learnt some lessons from a passionate and motivated scientist who had clearly shown everyone how to make a difference in this troubled world. No, I don't think I could motivate myself to devote all my life to pursuing a single dream as Dr. Galdikas had. Visiting Camp Leakey was also not just a tick mark on my bucket list. I was very glad that I had made it here. It had left a mark in my heart forever and I needed that above and beyond my thirst for wilderness.

Our next destination was Sekonyer village. But we still had one more trip to make i.e. to check Rimba Lodge with Desi. She very much wanted to do that and we didn't need to take any detour. It was down the same river on our way back. So, it was an easy trip. It was early afternoon when we anchored next to the lodge. For me, it was one more place to visit, however, for Desi, it was her living. Once we docked, she took the lead. We met the staff there and

Desi introduced herself. She asked if the staff could give us a short tour of the lodge and the facilities. Desi from 'Adventure Indonesia' carried some weight and the management understood the business.

"Not a problem," responded a staff member and showed us around.

I must admit, it was quite a comfortable place to spend a night or two in the middle of nowhere. This reminded me of Tharn Thong Lodge on the outskirts of Chiang Mai in Thailand. It always had a special place in my heart. Nestled in the lovely rolling hills of Northern Thailand, it was a perfect place to unwind. The landscape and ambience of the Rimba Lodge were totally different and I was not comparing the two. But an opportunity to spend one night at the lodge was very tempting, no doubt. It was a very quiet place and within walking distance from the swamp, just next to the wilderness. But I had chosen to spend the nights in a boat in the middle of nowhere and that was indeed a different kind of experience. I would probably get other opportunities to spend a few nights at the lodge sometime in the future. But I would not trade my choice of the boat with the lodge. Not a chance! No, there were no regrets.

We toured the lodge for half an hour and Desi liked the place.

"Shall we?" Desi asked when she came out to the lobby.

"You mean heading out? Are you done?"

"Yup!" she seemed to be happy with her usual smile.

We returned to the boat. The captain started the engine and we headed out to our last destination, Sekonyer village.

Sekonyer village and my last night in Borneo

S ekonyer village… what a lovely name! No, I wouldn't have missed a chance to visit such a peaceful and friendly village. That was where I found a rare opportunity to meet the people who live in the middle of the wilderness in Borneo and make it their home. I strongly believe that a place is always characterized by its people. My journey in Borneo would not have been complete until I had met the happy and contented locals in this village, nestled in the Borneo jungle and far away from the rest of the world. It always amazes me, especially in the rural areas, that some people have so little but their lives are so filled with laughter and happiness.

"Use your smile to change the world. Don't let the world change your smile," I thought. Missing Sekonyer was out of the question.

We arrived at the village in the late afternoon. To be honest, the place didn't look that impressive from a distance when we were getting out of the boat. Once we entered the village with our guide, my opinion changed. The village had two paved roads which intersected with each other and houses were built on both sides of the roads. They were not congested. Most houses were spacious with either a garden or a small yard in front of them. Some were made of brick and others of bamboo. Our guide told us that sometimes the houses get flooded with water from the swamps when there is too much rain. Given that the region gets a heavy dose of downpours, I wondered how the people managed to survive there. The village was nowhere close to any civilization but interestingly they had electricity. I noticed that there were a few street lamps that lit up for 3-4 hours in the evening, powered by a small electric generator run on diesel. The only grocery store that provided supplies to the villagers was at the village entrance and it gets its supplies once in a while from Pangkalan Bun. There was a primary school too and I was impressed by how well it was maintained. On the whole, I must say that the village was independent and self-sufficient. Above all, the people seemed to be happy. Kids were playing outside and a grandma was walking on the road with her two grandchildren. At our request, the group happily sat down on a bench under a tree for a photo op. It was amazing how people lived happily in such total isolation, surrounded by swamps, grassy lands, and miles of wilderness. Though I did wonder about what happened to them when people fell sick. I was sure that they must have certain arrangements for such situations.

"Look at how cute the kid is," said Desi and pointed towards a child sitting on her mother's lap.

The mother, a young girl in her twenties, was sitting on a porch with her child. She gave us a beautiful smile when we passed her home. She was so friendly! She invited us inside her home. She could see that we were tourists and was eager to show us around. It was so nice and we felt at home in her company! Often I find that the further people live from civilization, the more civilized they are. Isn't that ironic? Perhaps there is something wrong with how we define a civilized society.

No, we couldn't communicate with the family, not even Desi could. They did not speak Bahasa but a local dialect. As our guide chose to wait outside, there was no interpreter. But language was not a barrier for us, we managed it. Inside the house, the lifestyle was a very basic one with a bare minimum of living arrangements. But they were a happy family and that was all that mattered. I wouldn't have missed this rare opportunity to meet such a lovely family full of joy in this wilderness. It was so refreshing to be greeted by a friendly, young and loving mother. I will never forget that.

We took a leisurely walk on our way back to the boat. An elderly person was sitting outside his house. He smiled at us as we passed by. We smiled back and waved at him. He stood up and beckoned us to visit him. We thus had an opportunity to meet another local!

"How come these people are so friendly?" I wondered.

I suppose the villagers there looked forward to the new company due to their isolation from Pangkalan Bun, the nearest township. The elderly couple lived on their own. One of their sons lived close by and the other worked in Pangkalan Bun and visited his parents once in a while. The elderly lady showed us the mats she had knitted from dry grass to make a living. Again it was an eye-opener about how little one can have to live and still lead a happy life. I have seen this over and over again in other parts of the world, in the rural areas in Vietnam, Thailand and India, just to name a few. Every time I felt ashamed comparing their lifestyle with our materialistic greed. This once again reminded me that it is not our need, but our greed which kills our soul.

The elderly lady requested us to observe her knitting skills. She was obviously proud of them. We sat down and watched her knit a mat which was half finished. It was fascinating! Perhaps she had expected that we would buy a couple of mats from her. I wished I could, but it would have been impossible for me to carry the bulky mats with me during my travels. I don't think Desi or Kadek needed one either. Instead, I offered the lady some cash as a gift, but she didn't accept it. Was I taken aback? Perhaps a bit, because tourists like us often take things for granted and we need to be reminded from time to time that money cannot buy everything in this world. I really admired her integrity. Most of the people in the village worked or were connected to the palm oil industry but surely not this elderly couple. The industry didn't need them. However, their hand-to-mouth existence couldn't steal their beautiful smile and they had found their way to survive. We said goodbye to them and continued our exploration of the village.

We wanted to check the grocery store on our way out. It was the last landmark while exiting the village. The store was near the end of a paved road close to where we had docked our boat. We heard some music being played at a distance. When we came near the store, we found that the store owner playing a guitar-like instrument made from bamboo. Some of the locals were just spending their idle time chatting while sitting on a bench. We were curious and stood there watching them. The owner saw us standing near the entrance and greeted us in Bahasa. Bingo! Kadek blended with the group right away, chatting in their language. Before we realized what was happening, to our delight, Kadek quickly joined the group and started playing the instrument! All of us joined the fun... I didn't know Kadek could play instruments so well. We spent some more time in the store enjoying the company before heading to the boat.

It was near sundown when our boat revved up its engine for the day's final run. We were to sail near Tanjung Puting before we anchored for the night. We settled on the deck while the boat sailed along the Sekonyer river. A quiet dusk was falling across the rainforest and the wetlands. The wildlife present during the daytime was making room for the creatures of the night. We were all absorbed in our thoughts. It had been a splendid journey for the last two days and we were sad to see it come to an end. As the dusk slowly settled in under the dense trees and the wetlands, it made our mood more sombre. Suddenly, the boat slowed down, coming to a complete halt. There was another boat in front of us, which was also not moving. We stopped.

What was the matter? Our guide came up running to the starboard side. We were all jolted from our thoughts. It was unusual at this hour!

"Something must have happened," I murmured.

Then we saw it. A tree had fallen across the narrow river blocking the way ahead. Crews from other boats were already down in the water with a couple of hand-saws to cut the tree and clear the way. Our guide also jumped in the water to help the others. The water appeared dark in the fading twilight, but I was sure that it was by no means clean. Hats off to the crews! They swam in the murky water and cut the branches in the looming darkness. There were a few others who watched out for the crocs to ensure their safety. The light was fading fast and it was not an easy job to cut off a large tree in such conditions, especially with just a pair of hand saws. Other boats that came behind us were all stalled. The torches were lit and the crews raced to clear the tree from the path before nightfall. Once it gets dark, it would be almost impossible to work in the water with limited resources. I was holding my high-power torch for the folks working laboriously. We stood there and helplessly watched the crew risking their lives in the croc-infested dirty water. We all knew if they hadn't, we would have been stuck there all night. I wanted to do something, anything, to help the crews. But apart from holding the torch, there was little I could do. I was ashamed of myself. I realized that I was just a typical urban character who even couldn't jump into the murky water to give those guys a hand! Once again it proved how hopeless we city dwellers are in a crisis like this!

Hooray, the team finally did it and cleared the tree just before nightfall. We were worried because we were all going to fly out the next day and we didn't want to get stranded. I was sure there were others like us on the other boats too. Thank God, the crews rescued us from an ordeal. Hats off to them!

Kadek and Desi went to bed early right after dinner. They were tired. I climbed up to the upper deck to soak up another night in the wilderness. This was my last night in Borneo, my last chance to feel the wilderness at night and embrace its beauty for the last time. Yes, I knew it would all be a memory when I went back and an unforgettable experience of a lifetime. I didn't have any idea whether I would ever return to Borneo in the future! Maybe, maybe not. I just embrace the present moment and treasure my past. Yes, this was my night.

It was around 9:30 pm and the world was pitch dark around me. The night sky full of stars silently blanketed the surrounding wilderness. I settled down near the handrail on a small chair. I looked around, there was only darkness. I strained my eyes to see across the swamps but there was nothing.

"Hello darkness, my old friend..." I mused in a low voice so as to not to disturb the nightlife around me.

Slowly I got absorbed in the concert of hundreds of nightly creatures, the sound of monkeys hooting and barking, and the chirping of night birds. I was deeply absorbed. My solitude broke like shattered glass when I heard a large splash in the swamp followed by a scream. I jumped out of my chair and quickly grabbed my torch. Must be a croc grabbing its prey. It was near our boat. I flashed my high-power torch into the swamp but couldn't see anything. The light faded away in the rising mist from the swamp. At one time, the screaming stopped and the splashing in the water died down. The night birds continued to chirp 'ti-ti-ti' and the sound of crickets came from a distance. All was normal just like a few minutes ago. I sighed. A life had ended and that too in an obscure part of the world in a swampy wilderness. The world wouldn't cry. Another life must have been born somewhere else in the world right at that moment. Circle of life? I didn't know. I looked up at the sky. It was a clear night. Orion was blinking at me, its bright belt flashing. I was told as a child that when loved ones pass away, they become stars in the sky.

"Is it true?" I asked myself. No one believes it today. But I wanted to believe it at that moment.

My father used to say, "Embrace the wilderness, travel the world, and don't keep any regrets, my son."

I looked at the stars and whispered, "Yes Father, I won't have any regrets."

It was past midnight. The rhythm was broken. A life had ended near me that night. I was in no mood to sit down there after the incident.

"Good night, Father."

"Yes my son, 'Take only memories, leave only footprints,'" he whispered in my ears from his abode in the Milky Way.

I climbed down the stairs and went to bed. But I couldn't take my mind off the fact that a life had been lost only a hundred feet away, just a few minutes ago.

The next morning, I told the group at the breakfast table about the previous last night.

"Really?" Desi looked at me wide-eyed, her mouth half open, chewing her toast.

"Yeah, a croc grabbed a monkey," said the guide in a flat tone.

I looked at him. There was no expression on his face as though it was normal. Life goes on. Nobody knew and no one cared. Circle of life, indeed. I sighed!

Surabaya – my last stop

We flew out from Pangkalan Bun early in the afternoon the next day. Desi and Kadek had to catch their flight to Yogyakarta and I was to fly to Surabaya, my last stop before heading home. Their flight was a few hours ahead of mine. I came to the airport to see them off. No, there was no easy way to say goodbye. Our fun-filled days of spending time together had come to an end, but it made a bond between us that was sealed forever. That being said, it was painful to part from them. There is a saying, *'Goodbye is painful only when you know you will never say hello again.'* No, I didn't want to believe in that, not at that moment. I sighed! We will live thousands of miles apart, but I will say 'hello' to them, always! I'll always remember the small things we did together. Simple things, like hiking in the woods or sharing a bug repellant or helping each other cross a puddle, and having breakfast together on the boat. All these memories would become treasures. How could I ever forget the time when the three of us joked and laughed in lighter moments sitting in the darkness, chatting around the breakfast table, enjoying the wilderness from the cabin rooftop? No, I cannot.

We hugged each other and said goodbye. I held Desi's hands and asked, "So this is it?"

Desi didn't reply but gave her beautiful innocent smile. I knew how she felt.

I shook my head and told her, "No, this is the beginning; the beginning of our ever-lasting friendship."

Desi was still smiling, her eyes glistening with tears.

Then finally she whispered, "It better be. I hate goodbyes. I'm better at 'hello.'"

Then she turned around and started walking to the security gate, perhaps to hide her tears from me.

Did this separation bring some tears to my eyes? Yes, I had felt my eyes becoming blurry and a lump in my throat. I watched them slowly walk past the security gate. Desi turned around one last time and waved goodbye! I waved back. Desi told me a couple of days ago she and Kadek were going to get married soon. I knew I wouldn't be able to attend their wedding, but my thoughts would always be there with them. They got married the following year and now they have a lovely child. We are still in touch.

I had some more time to kill before my flight was to leave in the afternoon so I asked the driver to go back to Pangkalan Bun. I had hardly seen the town. We drove around the township and visited the fishing village. I wanted to have a feel of the laid-back lifestyle of the sleepy town. It was a whirlwind tour, but it was productive. In two hours, I visited the only shopping complex in town, government offices, residential areas, and the marketplace. I even used a rudimentary toilet in the fishing village before heading out to the airport. I was content that I had made this the last bit of my tour.

I flew to Surabaya to meet my good friend Ninik. No, I didn't have any special agenda there. This was my last stop in Indonesia before flying out of the country en route to Kuala Lumpur. I could fly out to Kuala Lumpur from any other airport close to Pangkalan Bun. But I couldn't leave without meeting Ninik. To me, Surabaya means Ninik and my story will not be complete unless you get to know her.

Let me rewind a bit here. I came to know Ninik through a friend of mine in Canada. Actually, in the early stages of planning, I was toying with the idea of making a day trip to Mount Bromo, the famous active volcano in East Java. Apparently, watching the sunrise from it is spectacular. I checked the map. The approach road to the hiking trail had easier access from the city of Surabaya as compared to other towns. That was when I first got in touch with Ninik. Later, I studied the route carefully and I realized that it was too far to make a day trip. It takes more than a day for a return trip from Surabaya to Mount Bromo. One needs to halt overnight at Mount Bromo to view the sunrise. I knew that I could not afford another extra day. So I dropped the plan.

But I wanted to meet Ninik regardless as we became friends. I decided to make a stopover in Surabaya on my way back from Borneo and I was glad that I made the decision. What a lovely lady she was with a simple lifestyle! Even before I started my journey to Indonesia, she was advising me almost daily on tips for a safe trip with clear 'dos and don'ts.' Ninik was overly cautious and wanted to make sure that I didn't end up in any trouble when in Surabaya.

"No way, don't stay in this hotel. I want you to be safe," she cautioned me when I told her I was planning to spend the night in a budget hotel in Surabaya.

"Ok, fine," I told her and booked for one night in Holiday Inn instead.

"I will make sure we have a car with the safest driver when you are here," Ninik told me.

I laughed and said, "Ninik, I will be in Surabaya just for one night. Any car will do." Then I added, "You know, I am just coming to see you. I don't have any other travel plans."

"Oh yes, I know that. But you need to be safe. And I will pick you up from the airport," she insisted.

She was as protective as a mother hen and wanted to make sure that her good friend was safe. Isn't that lovely? It tells a lot about a person. So I left it to her to decide on the stay and other plans. I was totally relaxed when I took my flight from Pangkalan Bun to Surabaya. I had no stress since I knew I was in good hands.

Surabaya is the third largest city in Indonesia after Jakarta and Bekasi. Bekasi is a commuter city close to Jakarta, so the people from Bekasi have close ties with it. But Surabaya is a port city on its own. It has strategic, commercial and industrial importance. It is a vibrant metropolis with close to three million people living within the city limits. The population of greater Surabaya is close to ten million making it the second most populous city in Indonesia after Jakarta. It's too bad that I didn't have time to explore the city's vibrant lifestyle, but I decided to make the most of my one evening with Ninik.

It was a short flight to Surabaya, just over an hour from Pangkalan Bun. The Kalstar flight descended while coming out of the clouds. From my window seat, I could see the sprawling city on both sides of the Kalimas river down below. Shortly after, the aircraft touched down at the Juanda International Airport. I picked up my luggage and came out to the arrival terminal. There she was, waiting for me anxiously in the arrival lounge. I could see great relief on her face when she saw me coming out of the arrival gate.

"Hello Ninik," I greeted her with a smile.

"Are you ok?" was the first question she asked me.

"Why shouldn't I be? It was a short flight, Ninik," I laughed.

"No, you went to Borneo, so I was worried."

"Come on, Ninik. Relax! I am not the only one who travels to Borneo. I am fine. Let's go."

"Sure, the car is waiting outside."

"Thanks, Ninik. What is the plan?"

"Let's go to your hotel first and you can check in. Then we can head out a bit."

"Sounds like a plan!"

We walked to our car waiting outside the arrival terminal. After dumping my luggage into my room at Holiday Inn, I quickly returned to the main lobby where Ninik was waiting patiently for me. I looked up at the sky as we came out of the hotel. It wouldn't be long before dusk set in and it was humid and cloudy.

"You know, Ninik. Let's not stretch ourselves. I just want to spend some quality time with you. So whatever we can cover at a short distance is fine with me," I told her.

Surabaya was a big city, a sprawling metropolis that was home to a large Chinese community and a thriving Chinatown. The city's large metropolitan area also holds an Arab quarter which has an old mosque that was built back in the 15th Century. So there was a fair amount of history to how the city became what it is today. There was plenty to see in the city, but there was too little time. I just wanted to relax with Ninik, not run around all over the place. I already had my hectic run in the last ten days.

"Well, perhaps we can start with a quick visit to my school," she said.

The soft-spoken lady was a school teacher and she was eager to show me her school first. Why not? That has been her achievement in all these years and of course, her pride. I was all in for it. What would be a better opportunity to learn about local culture than visiting a children's school?

"That sounds fantastic, Ninik! Let's go then."

I was ready to move. As always, I was impatient. She smiled at me. Ninik was a patient lady and since she was a trained school teacher, she knew how to handle a bad student like me!

"Let me explain a bit first," Ninik told me calmly and continued, "On our way, we will stop momentarily at the Suroboyo Monument."

"What about it?" I wanted to know a bit more. It would help my blog for sure.

"It's a statue. 'Suro' means shark and 'Boyo' means crocodile. It's a monument that represents the city of Surabaya. I just want to show it to you. There is no need to spend much time there, it will be on our way. Besides, it's next to the zoo and there will be traffic."

"As you suggest, Ninik, you are the best! I'm game."

"I also want to show you a beautiful bridge we have in Surabaya, the famous Suramadu bridge."

"Looks like everything in Surabaya starts with 'Sur' Ninik," I couldn't resist a pun to lighten the mood. Ninik just smiled at me.

"Tell me more about the bridge, Ninik. Why is it so special?"

"Well, Suramadu bridge is the longest bridge in South East Asia. It connects Surabaya with Madura over the Strait of Madura."

"How long is it?"

"It's 5.4 kms long."

Wow! That was a long bridge alright. We were chatting as walked to our car. I checked my watch. It was only 4:30 pm, we had plenty of time. So we headed to Ninik's school. Our car snaked along the crowded roads from the hotel and we briefly stopped to see the beautiful Suroboyo monument. It was rush hour, so we drove through some busy intersections until we entered a relatively quiet residential neighbourhood. Ninik's school was there. School hours were long over and the students had already gone home. She led me inside the school and proudly showed me around. The shy and soft-spoken lady had every reason to be proud. I come from an academic family myself and I have always had tremendous respect and admiration for people in this profession. They are nation builders.

Traffic had increased by the time we headed to the bridge and dusk had already settled over the city leaving a thin film of haze in the air. We drove over the bridge until we came to the other end that connects Madura and turned around. I must say, it was a beautiful bridge with double lanes on both sides. Bright halogen lamps cut through the thin haze giving the bridge an ultra-modern appearance. Ninik told me that the people of Surabaya were proud of it.

"*And rightly so,*" I thought. "Where to next, Ninik?" I asked aloud.

"How about we stop for a while at Sanggar Agung Temple?" Ninik seemed to have chalked out the evening plans long ago.

"What about it?"

"You will be able to see the fusion of Chinese and Hindu cultures in the temple."

"*That's interesting,*" I thought.

Indonesia surprised me over and over again. It had shown how a predominantly Muslim country can live in harmony with other cultures and traditions from other faiths. I had seen that in Bali. Well, let's keep Bali aside for a moment because the predominant religion there is Hinduism. Let's take Yogyakarta. The Borobodur and Prambanan Temples were built in the Buddhist and Hindu eras and have been preserved by a secular Indonesian Government. Officially, the government recognizes six different religions. So I was not surprised, but I was curious when Ninik suggested that we visit the temple. In my mind, it made a perfect mosaic of a multicultural society coming from different faiths. Ninik patiently showed me around the temple. Indeed, the sculptures of Ganesh and other Hindu deities were perfectly maintained with full respect along with other Asian religious icons. Like us, hundreds of visitors flocked to the temple every day in the Pantai Ria amusement park. It was impressive!

We ended the day with a lovely dinner in a quiet restaurant and the driver dropped me to the hotel after we called it a night. I was tired from travelling all day and it didn't take me long to drift into sleep.

"*Today is my last day in Indonesia*," this was the first thought that came to my mind as soon as I woke up.

After taking a shower and finishing breakfast I quickly walked around the neighbourhood, close to the hotel. That was my usual routine wherever I travelled. I tried to get a vibe of the place, no matter how brief it was. Once back at the hotel, I quickly packed my luggage, checked my travel documents and headed to the elevator. Yes, this was it! This was the final hour of my remarkable trip to Indonesia. I felt sad as I went to the front desk to check out. Once the formalities were over, I waited in the lobby for Ninik to pick me up. She was on time.

As I greeted her, I was equally surprised and touched when she brought me some mangoes. Yes, it was a farewell gift from a soft-spoken lady, my kind-hearted friend Ninik who had looked after me since I arrived in Surabaya. She handed me the mangoes and she was visibly sad to see me go. I put the mangoes in my backpack and hugged her. The pack of mangoes was a very unusual gift, but a precious one. It was priceless! This came with her touch of love and friendship and that was all that mattered. There is nothing in this world which is more precious than the gift of love and friendship. I had been fortunate enough to be blessed with that all along during my footsteps around the world.

I was waiting in the departure lounge after an emotional parting from Ninik. Yes, it was the end of an epic journey that I had dreamt of all along. I was fortunate enough to make this journey and I am proud to share my story with you all. As I closed my eyes—Desi and Kadek, Gonzalez, our guide in Borneo, Ninik in Surabaya—all their faces appeared vividly in my mind with the pain of leaving them still fresh.

There are certain debts in our life that we can never pay back, we can only acknowledge them. These are the debts that I will carry with me forever, the love and friendship of people, and acts of kindness showered by so many along my footsteps. They embraced me with their affection and friendship. They created a permanent bond in my heart. They had guided me at each step wherever I travelled and had protected me from all dangers. How can I ever pay back this debt? Never! I felt a lump in my throat and my vision blurred. I heard the announcement for departure and slowly dragged myself to the departure gate with a heavy heart. I boarded the plane and showed my boarding pass to the flight attendant who greeted me at the gate. I found my seat and fastened the seat belt. I did everything mechanically, like a robot. My heart was somewhere else. I had left a piece of me with my friends who I had left behind, and who had shared my laughter and my fun.

The Air Asia flight took off on that gloomy afternoon. I was on my way to Kuala Lumpur. It was the end of a remarkable journey that I will always remember. I gazed through the window to get a last glimpse of a country that I had fallen in love with. I saw the canvas of a sprawling city by the sides of the Kalimas river. It was fading away fast on that cloudy afternoon. As we climbed higher, Surabaya slowly disappeared below the cloud.

"Goodbye Indonesia," I whispered and sighed deeply.

My mind was far away roaming in the Borneo jungle. I could see the sun setting behind the tall trees, dark shadows falling on Sekonyer river, the proboscis monkeys sitting on top of the trees, the orangutans climbing down the trees to grab bananas at Camp Leakey, and the young woman sitting on the doorstep with her child in Sekonyer village, greeting us with a smile. All these images were passing in front of my eyes like a slideshow. The image that my father had painted in my childhood dream had become real in the jungles of Borneo.

"Thank you, Father," I said.

He smiled at me and whispered, "Life is a finite journey, my son. Make it happen and leave no regrets."

"Yes, Father," I said, leaning back and closing my eyes.

The End

Semarang Airport

*Pangkalan Ban,
Borneo*

Welcome to Borneo

Kumai River – Heading out to Borneo wilderness

Sekonyer River – deep in the wilderness

A moment with our guide

Camp Leakey, with Kadek and Desi

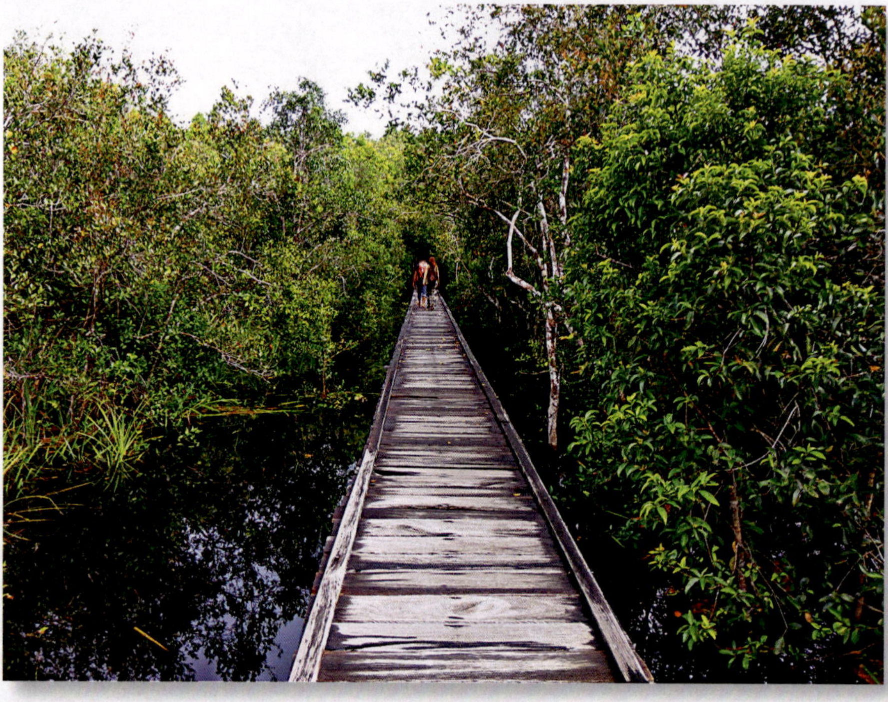

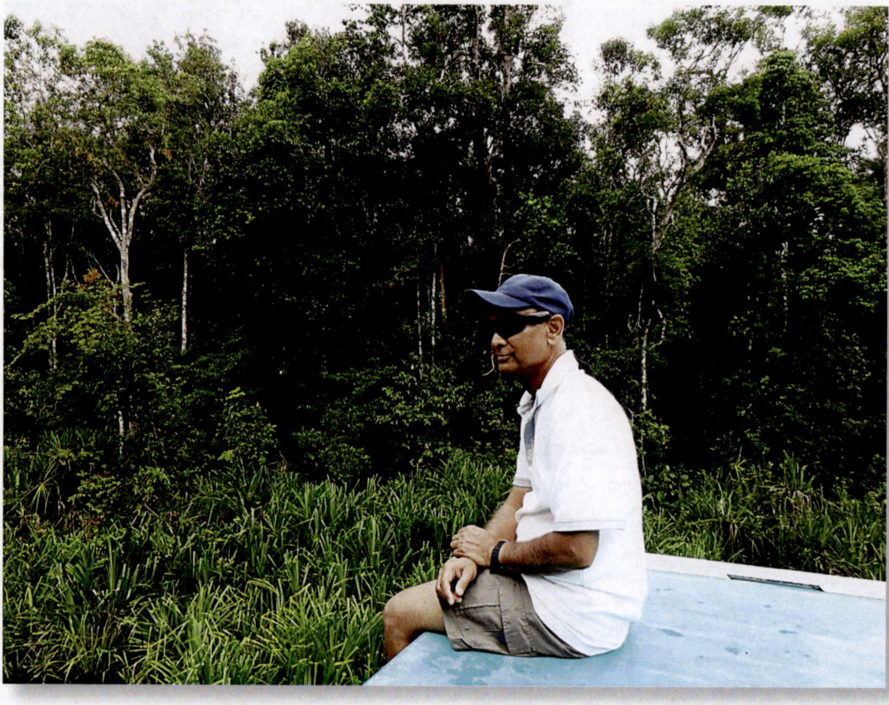

Dr. Galdikas, founder of Camp Leaky

Trekking orangutans

*Happy families in
Sekonyer Village*

A Village school

Kadek playing an instrument

Goodbye Borneo!

Surabaya

My friend Ninik, humble but a proud teacher

A Hindu deity in Surabaya

Leaving Surabaya